Modern Lutheran Theology

Modern Lutheran Theology

Volume One

Alexandra Glynn

Foreword by Mika Kallunki

WIPF & STOCK · Eugene, Oregon

MODERN LUTHERAN THEOLOGY
Volume One

Copyright © 2017 Alexandra Glynn. All rights reserved. Except for brief quotations in critical publications or reviews, no part of this book may be reproduced in any manner without prior written permission from the publisher. Write: Permissions, Wipf and Stock Publishers, 199 W. 8th Ave., Suite 3, Eugene, OR 97401.

Wipf & Stock
An Imprint of Wipf and Stock Publishers
199 W. 8th Ave., Suite 3
Eugene, OR 97401

www.wipfandstock.com

PAPERBACK ISBN: 978-1-5326-0409-6
HARDCOVER ISBN: 978-1-5326-0411-9
EBOOK ISBN: 978-1-5326-0410-2

Manufactured in the U.S.A.   FEBRUARY 16, 2017

The King James Version (KJV) is used throughout these writings. Where there is a slight divergence, it is my own translation idea.

Contents

Foreword by Mika Kallunki | *vii*

The robe of righteousness | 1
To believe as a child | 2
Peter's exhortation to us | 3
Blind people | 5
Casting us out | 7
Good works in us | 9
Sowing to the flesh and feeding it | 11
Love the stranger | 13
Hypocrites | 15
The children of this world are wiser | 17
He thinks | 20
Shimei | 22
Love and doctrine | 24
Note that man | 27
Only us | 30
Among the gods | 32
Preaching from envy and strife | 34
Death is swallowed up in victory | 37
Choice | 43
Oxen | 45
The hardening of Pharaoh's heart | 46

CONTENTS

The altar and the lamb | 50
I am not the Christ | 53
The fruits of repentance | 55
Lest ye be judged | 58
The lost sheep of the house of Israel | 60
Moses and the rock | 62
The work of theology | 65
Why do bad things happen? | 68
The sin of wanting | 70
Openly and publicly | 72
Comments on Genesis translations | 75
The secrets of men | 82
Visitation for a nation or people | 86
Women as priests | 88
The word "law" in the Scriptures | 90
Have mercy on me | 94
Ministers gone astray | 96
The church law of Christ | 98
Compassion on heretics | 101
The imagination | 103
Your sin will find you out | 105
Thanks and praise | 107
The text feeds | 109
Makeup and earrings | 111
The end of the book of Judges | 113
To never have forgiveness | 115
Jacob and Laban and Esau | 117

Foreword

The best way to be exposed to the theology of the Laestadian Lutherans is through their sermons. So below is a transcribed sermon given in 2014 on Luke 7:36–50.

JESUS HAD BEEN INVITED to a meal at the home of a Pharisee. Luke tells earlier how Jesus was also invited to publicans' and tax collectors' homes for a meal. The connection to a meal was an indication of great friendship and hospitality. A little earlier in the same chapter Luke told how John the Baptist came, and since he didn't eat bread or drink wine, they said that he had an evil spirit in him. Jesus went on to say that the son of man has come, he eats and drinks, and you say, what is this eater and drinker, a friend of publicans and sinners? Jesus did not reject the invitations that were given to him. Whoever invited him to a meal, whether a publican or a tax collector or a Pharisee, Jesus accepted the invitation.

This gospel text brings before us a woman and a man. One is a sinner and an evil woman, and the other is a respected, well-mannered Pharisee. It would seem from the situation described here that it was a "man's club" that had gathered together, to use a current saying. In other words, usually only men were gathered at these meals; women had no reason to be there. But something extraordinary happened, very exceptional: a woman came into the company of men.

To understand this text it is good to know the background to give light into what is taking place in this room where they have gathered. The tables were not like what we have. The tables were low to the ground; there were three tables formed into a U-shape and you laid down on your side and the food was served in the middle. So they were gathered at the home of a Pharisee. Jesus may have been teaching in the synagogue of this locality and the Pharisees politely invited him to their home.

We have heard much about the Pharisees in the Bible. What kind of image do you have of a Pharisee? First you may have heard, as from the mouths of children, that they are hypocrites, and self-righteous, those Pharisees. And Jesus does even speak of this. Jesus tells that the teachers of the law and the Pharisees sit on the throne of Moses, but then he reminds us to do as they say and respect their teachings. Jesus did not say: do not listen to the Pharisees. He said: listen to them, but he continued: do not do according to their works, for they talk in one way and act in another way. They give great and heavy burdens, and they give them to others to carry, but they themselves will not lift a finger to help.

The Pharisees were a religious group of the Jews. Laymen and lower clergy were also involved, and they were like an opposition party to the Sadducees. They emphasized abiding by the law and traditions, the rules from their forefathers; they said that the law applies in all areas of your life, but in their own regulations they denied hypocrisy. They said that in no way can you be a hypocrite. And they were serious in their faith.

When we think of this way of thinking of the Pharisees, hypocrisy, do we find it in our time? Maybe I have at this time the temptation to point my finger at other people, at other awakening movements, at different churches and organizations. I point my finger and say that they surely are Pharisees. Truly it is so. But do we dare to, as relating to this gospel portion, look closer? May there also be found in our midst the thoughts of the Pharisees? Self-righteousness, mercilessness, hardheartedness? Do we dare take a step closer? In you and in me, are these ways found in me? This is where this gospel text brings us. How does the way of the Pharisees look here in this story? The Pharisee, who invited Jesus, saw what the woman did. "If this man were a prophet he would know what kind of woman is touching him. The woman is a sinner." The Pharisees were astonished, everyone knew these things; rumors had spread throughout the village that she is such a woman, a prostitute. Stay away from her, do not let her come near. Is there something familiar about this? Are you ever in a situation where you are astonished about something, astonished about some person, you look the other way, you avoid certain people? When somebody comes to you or me to tell us, "Have you heard about so and so? Have you heard what he has done or has not done?" How do you react? The temptation to judge what others have done lives deeply within us all. The temptation is to measure different sins, small and large ones. Have you ever been in a situation where someone has come to tell a juicy story? Have we stopped and asked the person who told the story to us if they have approached that person directly? Do we ask them, "Why did you come talk to me? Have you talked personally to this person?" The gospel of Matthew encourages us, in the eighteenth chapter, to act according to the church law of Christ. Maybe we don't start spreading rumors, but we nicely say that we are concerned about her, we need to care for her. There is a fault even in a tone of love if we do wrongly, if we go around to our friends, our brothers, our sisters, with these stories and we don't go straight to the person, we don't ask what kinds of burdens they are under in their travels, if we only listen to rumors. God's word, his commandments, remind even us children of God: "Do not bear false witness against your neighbor." Jesus himself says very seriously in another connection: "If you see a sliver in your brother's eye, but you don't notice that in your own eye is a log, how can you say to your brother, 'I will take the sliver from your eye,' when in your own eye is a log? You hypocrites, take the log from your own eye first, then you can see to take the sliver from your brother's eye." This word of God is directed to you and me. Nobody is outside these words.

In this gospel text, in its central theme, there is also greeting and not greeting. Greeting someone is a tradition in many cultures.

Greeting is important for acknowledging the other. The duty of the slave was to wash the feet of the guests. Kissing one's cheek also was a tradition, or one might kiss the hand of an important guest. Also, olive oil was used to anoint the head of a distinguished guest. We have the tradition of shaking hands, which is a very beautiful tradition and suitable in our culture. Hugging has also become more common, nodding your head, saying, "Hi." How was it for this evil woman? Regardless of how others viewed her?

This woman came behind Jesus, came and cried. What does this crying relate? We could say that they were tears of regret, but maybe there was more. There could have been more . . . they could have been tears of joy, that she had heard, seen Jesus speaking and had believed that here is her Lord and Savior, that here is her Lord and Savior who does not drive her away. So many had driven her away, so many had shown the rejecting hand, as if saying, "When you change your way of life then you can be forgiven." But how did the Lord Jesus react? In a completely different way. The idea that we would first change our way of life, then we would be forgiven, comes from man. It comes from man's requirements and human-centered faith. The woman cried. Jesus' feet were wetted with her tears. She dried them with her hair and kissed them, and anointed them with alabaster ointment. The works of love came from faith.

Simon the Pharisee did not show any respect for the guest. We can imagine what it would be like to come to a house. We are invited as guest to some house, we come, we open the door ourselves, the host says nothing, we hang our jacket on a hook, go into the room. Nobody says anything. All avoid us. We find our own chair. This is how the Pharisee reacted. How is it at summer services? Here, joyful greetings are heard. We meet others that we haven't seen in years. God's peace. We have with joy greeted and talked with one another. Greetings have a very great significance. Sometimes the words may not even be heard but it is expressed from the look that I value you, it is good to see you. Even here it is good to see so many of my friends. At this moment there are many friends who have not made it to these services who listen on the radio or on the computer somewhere far away. Someone is on their sick bed; they may not even be able to listen, but there, far away, some friend is remembering her. They say, "Let's go visit," and they greet, bringing greetings of God's peace.

Jesus sent twelve disciples and said: when you go into a house, greet with the greetings of peace, wish them peace; if the guests are not ready to accept the greetings, then return. I thought about this yesterday when I was able to give communion along with many other pastors, and in the end it is said, when releasing, to all communion guests, "Go in the peace of God." How beautiful it is and how much significance there is in this greeting, "Go in the peace of God." It may be that greeting someone may be difficult in our daily lives, there are unfamiliar guests; sometimes we might mutter a greeting to someone, but yet take no notice of that person. We do not need to be ashamed, but many times we can be ashamed of greeting. What then if a friend does not greet you? It could be that he didn't notice you as he walked by. What if the friend does not greet you on purpose? Does he do as the Pharisees did in this story? What does it mean if someone does not greet you with God's peace? The message related is that you are not considered a believer. If some Christian decides that I will not greet that brother or sister because in my mind he is such a sinner, and that Christian tells others not to greet that person, then he is acting like the Pharisees in this story. We must ask ourselves seriously in connection to this: do we see inside the heart of another person? Jesus saw. But do we? In the same way we must ask seriously before the Word of God, do we see our own condition? Here it is reminded that it is good to learn the history of Christianity. It is good to remember all the beautiful and good, but it is good to learn where the faults/errors have come from, where have the heresies come from. In Christianity during the different phases, in the beginning phases and in the later phases, there have been Pharisees. Man becomes as if he is God. It is a very dangerous doctrine, that we as humans rise up to the level of God. May God protect us from this.

Simon the Pharisee thought that the woman was a sinner. Here in the middle of this story is a parable of two men who owed money to a lender, a different amount, 50 and 500 denarii. Both were big amounts. When they couldn't pay it back, the lender forgave them their debt; both debtors received it forgiven, both were shown grace. Although the host, Simon, was a debtor, he did not show love. How was it with this woman? She showed love the whole time. Love is the result when one experiences grace. This woman received all her sins forgiven, not just some of the sins, but all sins forgiven. She received a great amount of sins forgiven and she showed a great amount of love.

Love is a fruit of faith. Today, good service guests, have you received a little or much forgiven? How is it in the light of God's Word, how do we see our own situation? Is it not proclaimed to you and to me, to the congregation, all sins forgiven? When we remember how much I have been loved, how much I have been forgiven, don't we also want to forgive those little faults of our brothers and sisters? Surely the transgressions and faults can be burdensome, but ask and pray for power to have them forgiven.

Jesus did something very unusual. While he was eating at the home of a stranger he began rebuke the host. He said, "Look at this woman. When I came into your home you did not give me water to wash my feet, but she wet my feet with her tears and dried them with her hair. You did not greet me with a kiss, but she has been kissing my feet since I arrived. You did not anoint my head with oil, but she anointed my feet with ointment." Faith effects works of love. Love shows how we relate to those close to us. The Pharisees were offended by the woman. But even more, these Pharisees were offended by Jesus. The main person in this story is not the Pharisee, not even the woman, but the center-most is Jesus Christ. He does not reject the weak and wounded person. He receives that person and shows mercy. Maybe there is someone at services or listening who is rejected. Someone to whom it has been said, "You are not acceptable here. You are acceptable only when you are such and such a person." As people we may speak in this way. We may speak in this way in our homes or with families. I think about you mothers and fathers who may have several children, it is good when the kids help and learn good things in the family, take responsibility; but at the same time, I think of the older kids who help, and when the little ones need a lap, they are there. These older kids also need laps and love, all ages and sizes—we all hunger for love. As humans we may reject another person, but the king of the Kingdom of God, the Lord Jesus, does not reject.

At these services we have heard the good message, the joyous message, from the Lord Jesus Christ, to you who have been tried, who are like this woman, you who many times have been looked at and rejected, the Lord Jesus does not look in this way, he looks graciously, with value, with mercy. In the gospel of Luke, there is the portion where Peter denied Jesus three times before the rooster sang. The gospel tells that Jesus looked at Peter. We could imagine how Jesus looked at Peter, he who three times denied Jesus. Full of grace, full of love. The gospel tells how Peter went out and wept bitterly. This woman did not say anything in the house of the Pharisee, but her works told of her. We do not need long speeches, even though I have spoken long here, but in everyday life those small works of love to our friends and close ones, they have great significance.

We do not just examine the Word of God, but the Word examines us. Jesus looks graciously on us today, even though we may have gone to the place of the Pharisee, hardened, hypocritical. The son of God looks on us graciously and calls us as partakers of his grace. In the speakers meeting, in the introduction, was a question: is it enough if we preach only of Christ? One older speaker kept a speaking turn where he said there where Christ is, there is the Kingdom of God. That we would always preach the crucified and resurrected Lord Jesus Christ. For as sinful people we get comfort from no other place. At work at the hospital,—I will not tell personal stories for the sake of privacy, but this I can say,—that a person that is about to die (leave) becomes comforted only from the crucified and risen Lord Jesus Christ. But not only the one that is leaving, but even us who may have much of our life still to live, you also are comforted by faith that you can today believe that all of your sins are forgiven in Jesus' name and atoning blood. You can be of a secure mind that the Lord Jesus sees your difficulties; he sees everything. As Paul writes to the Corinthian congregation:

FOREWORD

I have not wanted to say anything more than the crucified Lord Jesus Christ. And Paul continues in another portion, that we do not proclaim ourselves but Jesus Christ, that he is the Lord. Lift up your hearts, hearers of the Word this evening, to believe sins forgiven in Jesus' name and blood. We can be secure traveling. Bless one another, bless with this most precious gospel that the Lord Jesus suffered and died and rose again on all of our behalf. He is the beginning and end of our faith. I want to also at the end ask if I may remain believing. I wish to remain believing with you. In Jesus' name, amen.

Mika Kallunki
a sermon given on Luke 7:36–50
transcribed into English by Jim Lehtola

The robe of righteousness

THE BIBLE RELATES THAT after Adam and Eve fell into sin, God clothed them with a robe to cover their shame: "Unto Adam also and to his wife did the Lord God make coats of skins, and clothed them" (Gen 3:21). This robe that covers the shame of man is also mentioned in the story of Noah's drunkenness: "And Shem and Japheth took a garment, and laid it upon both their shoulders, and went backward, and covered the nakedness of their father; and their faces were backward, and they saw not their father's nakedness" (Gen 9:23). The robe of righteousness is to cover nakedness (Ezek 18:7, 2 Cor 5:3–4, Rev 3:18, 16:15). It is white (Rev 3:5).

This robe of righteousness is pure and washed clean by Christ's own blood (Gen 49:11, Rev 7:14). We cannot add anything to this righteousness because our own righteousness is as a filthy rag (Isa 64:6). Aaron and the priests wore this robe of righteousness as a visible picture of Christ's perfection (Exod 28:2, Lev 6:10). In Isaiah this robe of righteousness is called the garment of praise (61:3, 11). It is also called "the righteousness of saints" since it becomes ours through faith (Rev 19:8). It is also called the "wedding garment" because we must have it on to be acceptable to the heavenly wedding (Matt 22:11–13). If we wear the filthy garment, we need to have it taken off and be clothed with the pure garment (Zech 3:3, Gen 35:2).

To believe as a child

WE KNOW THAT WE must be as a little child to enter into the kingdom of heaven (Mark 10:15). We also know that God has hidden his mysteries "from the wise and prudent, and has revealed them unto babes" (Matt 11:25). David says he is as a child (Ps 131:2). When Naaman was converted, his flesh became as a child's (2 Kgs 5:14). And we, as little children, want to be brought to Jesus, and receive the pure milk of the word (1 Pet 2:2). For children are the greatest in the kingdom of heaven (Matt 18:1–4).

The Bible also says that there is such a thing as being childlike in the wrong way. We are being childlike in the wrong way when we are ignoring the study of the Word (Heb 5:12–13). For we all know that little children do not study the Word of God because they do not know how to read. This is because they do not need to. They have perfect faith. But as they get older, they need more weapons to battle against the wiles of the enemy. And so God has given us his written Word, and he has also given us the ability to learn to read, and schools to go to learn in. God gives gifts in his congregation so we can learn his Word and not be as children "tossed to and fro, carried about with every wind of doctrine, by the sleight of men, and cunning craftiness, whereby they lie in wait to deceive" (Eph 4:14).

So let us heed the Word, and study it diligently. "Brethren, be not children in understanding. Howbeit in malice be ye children, but in understanding be men" (1 Cor 14:20).

Peter's exhortation to us

PETER SAYS THAT AS long as he is in this body, this tabernacle, he will use his time to stir up the others. That is, to incite them, to provoke them unto love and good works, as it says in Hebrews 10:24. Consider the verb "stir up." You stir up a fire, for example, when it is getting low, and it flames up once again. You stir up a pot every so often, so that what you are cooking doesn't congeal, or burn. It has to heat up, but it must not burn. After you stir the pot, it is fine for a while. Then you have to go back a little while later and stir it again. Then it is fine for a little while longer. In the same way, you stir up people who are lethargic so that they can pay attention when danger comes by.

I often think that we stir ourselves up every Sunday and every mid-week day that we go to services or go visiting or go to Bible Class. It helps us at the time, but we still have to go the next time and the next time, to keep ourselves from congealing.

To stir up is to provoke, to urge. Peter says he goes around stirring people up—that is his pastoral work. He exhorts, comforts, rebukes, reminds, consoles. These are his acts of love and good works. For when we come together to visit, or to look into God's Word, or to hear it preached, we are never learning anything new. Paul writes: "But as touching brotherly love ye need not that I write unto you; for ye yourselves are taught of God to love one another" (1 Thess 4:9). Why does he say "you do not need that I write to you" and yet he writes it to us? Because we forget. And so we have to exhort each other and tell each other the things that we already know but are always in danger of letting go of, of forgetting, of slipping from (Heb 2:1). This is what Peter says he does. He says: "I will not be negligent to put you always in remembrance of these things, though ye know them, and be established in the present truth" (2 Pet 1:12). For we are instructed and know, but we must re-know, we must be reminded, we must be made sure again. The gospel writer begins his gospel, explaining why he wrote it and why we must read the gospel. He says that it is so that "thou mightest know the certainty of those things, wherein thou hast been instructed" (Luke 1:4). We are certain, but we need to always be made more certain.

Because we have the Holy Spirit abiding in our hearts by faith, we already know: "But ye have an unction from the Holy One, and ye know all things" (1 John 2:20). But we get distracted by other things, as the parable says (Luke 8:14), and we wax cold, and our flesh gets in the way. And thus we do not do the Word, and we even forget what we have heard and know. But Jesus reminds us: "If ye know these things, blessed are ye if ye do them" (John 13:17). And the Holy Spirit in us, even as we tire and forget, still knows what is right, and reminds us in our heart: "Now we have received, not the spirit of the world, but the spirit which is of God; that we might know the things that are freely given to us of God" (1 Cor 2:12).

So may God help us, and stir us up and provoke us continuously through our brothers and sisters, as it is written: "And the Lord make you to increase and abound in love one toward another, and toward all men, even as we do toward you" (1 Thess 3:12). For it is also written: "Withhold not good from them to whom it is due, when it is in the power of thine hand to do it. Say not unto thy neighbor, 'Go, and come again, and to morrow I will give,' when thou hast it by thee" (Prov 3:27–28).

Blind people

IF YOU SAT DOWN to dinner with a blind person, would you mock his groping for a fork? Would you wonder why he makes a mess all over his shirt? Would you laugh at him if he tipped over his cup of milk? You would not. Why? Because you understand that the person sitting across from you is blind. They cannot see. Because they are blind, great compassion and help is shown to them.

Why then, I ask you, dear Christian, do you not treat people who are spiritually blind with the same compassion, with the same heart of help? Instead of being compassionate, we feel superior to the other one. We think: good for me, I know, and this other person, he sure is an idiot—he doesn't know even the things that are obvious and easy.

Do you see our error, dear Christian? Do you notice that Jesus never had the smug and superior attitude that we have towards those who are blind? He knew that they were deaf and dumb and blind and that they didn't even realize it. For every person in the natural world who is blind knows that he is blind. But the devil has caused the supreme blindness in those he has deceived. He has convinced them that, in fact, they see (John 9:39–41).

So let us look on those who are not of us as beloved of God and as possessed by the power of the wicked one, as Jesus did. Jesus "rebuked the foul spirit, saying unto him, thou dumb and deaf spirit, I charge thee, come out of him, and enter no more into him" (Mark 9:25). Notice that in this example Jesus isn't even speaking to the individual human being. He is speaking to the foul spirit that possesses the heart of the human being. Jesus is so sure that the problem in the person is the evil that owns the person, that reigns in him. The human being himself is dear, beloved, and to be pitied. When people of the world threw themselves into the fire, or foamed like lunatics, Jesus knew it was the devil, and rebuked the devil (Matt 17:18). Thus, again, the person was separated from the power that had held him in thrall, the wrongness, the lies. The Bible explains to us how we are to understand those who do not believe. It says they are in "the snare of the devil," and "are taken captive by him at his will" (2 Tim 2:26).

So let us be patient and compassionate and loving. Let us let our pride and flesh go—let us starve our flesh, for some devils do not come out of people except by fasting and prayer (Matt 17:21). For we are blind, and we know it, and therefore we see, by the Spirit, with eyes of faith. As it is written: "And in that day shall the deaf hear the words of the book, and the eyes of the blind shall see out of obscurity, and out of darkness" (Isa 29:18).

Christ, God's own son, leads us, the blind and the lame. Therefore we see, and leap rejoicing: "And I will bring the blind by a way that they knew not; I will lead them in paths that they have not known. I will make darkness light before them, and crooked things straight. These things will I do unto them, and not forsake them" (Isa 42:16). Let us remember that "the hearing ear, and the seeing eye, the Lord hath made even both of them" (Prov 20:12). And let us remember that it is also written of those who do not take hold of the promises of God:

> In them is fulfilled the prophecy of Esaias, which saith, "By hearing ye shall hear, and shall not understand; and seeing ye shall see, and shall not perceive. For this people's heart is waxed gross, and their ears are dull of hearing, and their eyes they have closed, lest at any time they should see with their eyes, and hear with their ears, and should understand with their heart, and should be converted, and I should heal them."

But we have received of grace the blessed portion: "But blessed are your eyes, for they see, and your ears, for they hear" (Matt 13:14–16).

Casting us out

In John 9:34 it says: "They answered and said unto him, 'Thou wast altogether born in sins, and dost thou teach us?' And they cast him out." Sometimes the children of God are cast out. When this happens, dear one, do not think it strange.

> Beloved, think it not strange concerning the fiery trial which is to try you, as though some strange thing happened unto you. But rejoice, inasmuch as ye are partakers of Christ's sufferings. That, when his glory shall be revealed, ye may be glad also with exceeding joy. If ye be reproached for the name of Christ, happy are ye. For the spirit of glory and of God resteth upon you. On their part he is evil spoken of, but on your part he is glorified (1 Pet 4:12–14).

It is written about those who say they are Christians, but are not, that God will make it clear to them and us and all the world what the true state of matters is:

> Behold, I will make them of the synagogue of Satan, which say they are Jews, and are not, but do lie; behold, I will make them to come and worship before thy feet, and to know that I have loved thee. Because thou hast kept the word of my patience . . . (Rev 3:9–10).

For it must always be that the devil tries to ruin the children of God. As it is written: "The wicked have drawn out the sword, and have bent their bow, to cast down the poor and needy, and to slay such as be of an upright way of life" (Ps 37:14).

When we are cast out, let us remember Jesus and say: "Behold, for peace I had great bitterness. But thou hast in love to my soul delivered it from the pit of corruption. For thou hast cast all my sins behind thy back" (Isa 38:17). And: "Hear the word of the Lord, ye that tremble at his word. Your brethren that hated you, that cast you out for my name's sake, said, 'Let the Lord be glorified.' But he shall appear unto your joy and they shall be ashamed" (Isa 66:5). For they cast us out in the name of God, and think that they do God great service in casting us out. Please remember, dear one, that they really do think that they serve God by being against us. This speaks to their blindness, and requires compassion on our part. Whoever is merciful will receive mercy, so let us be merciful to them, and to all people. For as it was with David, so it is with us: "They also that render evil for good are my adversaries, because I follow the good" (Ps 38:20).

Good works in us

WE ARE TO BE zealous of good works. David's works to Saul were done in Christ and thus were good works (1 Sam 19:4). We all do bad works by nature, but Christ in us does good works. Let us follow after these good works of Christ in us. For of ourselves we do evil (Ps 14:1). But Christ in us, by his Spirit, works in us and in others who are of Christ. So when we see good works in our fellow Christians, let us think that it is Christ in them that is shining forth, and not anything of the person. For that is the truth. Good works are Christ's good works in us that others see (Matt 5:16).

People don't like these good works that are done in Christ and attributed to him alone. Jesus said to the people: "Many good works have I shewed you from my Father, for which of those works do ye stone me?" (John 10:32). Now if Jesus had taken the credit for his own good works, the self-righteous would not have wanted to stone him. But since he gave glory to God, they wanted to stone him.

For we are God's workmanship. It is written: "For we are his workmanship, created in Christ Jesus unto good works, which God hath before ordained that we should walk in them" (Eph 2:10). Let no one forget this. We are created "unto good works." That is, to help other people. It is written: "A friend loveth at all times, and a brother is born for adversity" (Prov 17:17). We ought to study and learn when we are young especially, so that we can better help our neighbors, and be "thoroughly furnished unto all good works" (2 Tim 3:17). For "the good works of some are manifest beforehand, and they that are otherwise cannot be hid" (1 Tim 5:25).

It is written: "The righteous considereth the cause of the poor. But the wicked regardeth not to know it" (Prov 29:6). So let us remember the poor, the widow, the stranger. For it is even written that we are purified and made holy in order that we might not just *do* good works, but *be zealous* to do them: "[Christ] gave himself for us, that he might redeem us from all iniquity, and purify unto himself a special chosen people, zealous of good works" (Titus 2:14). And again: "This is a faithful saying, and these things I will that thou affirm constantly, that they which have believed in God might be careful to maintain good works. These things are good and profitable unto all men" (Titus 3:8). From my own experience, the reason good works profit me is that they keep me from doing other things that I should not be doing. Constantly keeping busy doing good works keeps me out of trouble. If I'm so busy helping others, how will I have time to be lazy and tempted and wander, and come to poverty (Prov 24:30–34)?

So, "let us consider one another to provoke unto love and to good works" (Heb 10:24) which are done in Christ, from a purified heart, giving all glory to God. For it is written: "Who is a wise man and endued with knowledge among you? Let him show out of a good conversation [a good way of life] his works with meekness of wisdom" (Jas 3:13). And it is also written that we should have our way of life be "honest among the Gentiles; that, whereas they speak against you as evildoers, they may by your good works, which they shall behold, glorify God in the day of visitation" (1 Pet 2:12). Notice, if you will, that here Peter, like Christ in the Sermon on the Mount, notes that good works are not for us to notice, for we don't even see them (Matt 25:38). But they are for others to notice. And we have this testimony from God in the Scriptures that they do notice, and maybe this will speak to them in some way and we will gain them. Who knows? "Hate the evil, and love the good, and establish judgment in the gate. It may be that the Lord God of hosts will be gracious unto the remnant of Joseph" (Amos 5:15).

Sowing to the flesh and feeding it

FROM GENESIS 47:23 WE read: "Then Joseph said unto the people, 'Behold, I have bought you this day and your land for Pharaoh; lo, here is seed for you, and ye shall sow the land.'" The idea of sowing seed is in the Bible often. Usually it is used to picture the sowing of the Word of God into the hearts of men. For we sow for six years, or, throughout the work week, until the everlasting Sabbath harvest (Exod 23:10, Lev 25:3-4). And we do not sow "mingled seed," but only the pure unmixed Word of God (Lev 19:19, Deut 22:9). And often we sow the seed weeping (Ps 126:5).

What we sow, we will reap (Gal 6:7). As it says: "Even as I have seen, they that plow iniquity, and sow wickedness, reap the same" (Job 4:8). Only God knows what will happen to that which we sow (Eccl 11:6). And we need first to break up the fallow ground, the hard hearts. The Word of God does this work in hearts (Hos 10:12). And we know that "he which soweth sparingly shall reap also sparingly, and he which soweth bountifully shall reap also bountifully" (2 Cor 9:6).

We want to sow to the Spirit, and not to the flesh. "For he that soweth to his flesh shall of the flesh reap corruption; but he that soweth to the Spirit shall of the Spirit reap life everlasting" (Gal 6:8). This sowing to the flesh question is one of the most important to keep in mind when we think of what the Bible is telling us about choices we make. For in the Bible we do not have specific answers to questions about celebrating Halloween, or going to certain entertainment places, or looking at certain things on our phones, or wearing certain items, or taking up certain hobbies. But we do have this broad warning: if we sow to the flesh, we will reap corruption. So we can ask, in any given situation, when I do this, or when I take this up, am I sowing to the flesh? And then we have our answer as to whether or not we want to keep doing what we are doing or thinking what we are thinking.

We do not want to feed the flesh. We want to starve it. Especially in difficult situations with our neighbors, when someone is in dire straits. For some demons are at work so powerfully in our neighbor, such as in the case of addictions, that Jesus says, fast (starve the flesh) and pray. This is our only hope with such people in such situations. Jesus said that "this kind goeth not out but by prayer and fasting" (Matt 17:21). So let us do as Daniel, and pray, and not sow to the flesh:

> And I prayed unto the Lord my God, and made my confession, and said, O Lord, the great and dreadful God, keeping the covenant and mercy to them that love him, and to them that keep his commandments; we have sinned, and have committed iniquity, and have done wickedly, and have rebelled, even by departing from thy precepts and from thy judgments (Dan 9:4–5).

Love the stranger

IN THE BIBLE WE are reminded: "Love the stranger, therefore, for you were strangers in the land of Egypt" (Lev 19:34). He does not only say "love the stranger." He says "love the stranger" and then he tells you why. He says: you were just like those strangers. At one time that was you, a stranger, in the land of Egypt, the land of the unrighteous. And the unrighteous shall not inherit the kingdom:

> Know ye not that the unrighteous shall not inherit the kingdom of God? Be not deceived: neither fornicators, nor idolaters, nor adulterers, nor effeminate, nor abusers of themselves with mankind, nor thieves, nor covetous, nor drunkards, nor revilers, nor extortioners, shall inherit the kingdom of God. And such were some of you; but ye are washed, but ye are sanctified, but ye are justified in the name of the Lord Jesus, and by the Spirit of our God (1 Cor 5:9–11).

I think sometimes that unbelief, Egypt, is difficult for childhood Christians to understand and remember. This is why we have to stand by what Scripture says, and know it well, and not go by what the first inclination of our heart is. For when we grow up as a childhood Christian we are preserved from so much. The fleshpots of Egypt are foreign to us, the worldly ways of talking, the things done for entertainment, the relationships between husband and wife, parents and children—all these things are like things that happen on another planet.

But the Bible says "you were strangers in the land of Egypt." So we have to constantly remind ourselves, I would be just like that, I would be just like those others, if God had not had mercy on me. I would be wearing all that strange adornment, I would be speaking that way and holding grudges. I would be a hater (Titus 3:3). I would be praying on the street-corners in stark self-righteousness. I would be in the drinking and entertainment venues of this world, a slave to my desires. I would never be in meekness instructing those who oppose themselves (2 Tim 2:25).

I have sometimes thought in connection with this text about loving the strangers that two of our beloved New Testament writers had their time in this world—Paul and Peter. So they understood what it had been like to be in darkness—they didn't have to imagine themselves in the shoes of the one who was not a Christian. They had lived it. "By the grace of God I am what I am," Paul confessed (1 Cor 15:10). Exactly. By the grace of God. We have a saying in English which is not from Scripture but captures the idea of Scripture so beautifully. We say this saying when we see a homeless person on the street, or when we see someone taking a hard fall into the fearsome places of this world: "There but for the grace of God go I."

Hypocrites

A HYPOCRITE IS AN actor. He is someone who is really one way but is pretending to be another. Luther often reminded us that what the law wants, the will never wants, unless it pretends to want it out of fear or love. We could discuss this saying in detail for a while. But I would like now only to direct your attention to the word Luther often uses, "pretend." People by nature don't want to be good or do good. When they seem to be good or do good, they are pretending to want to be that way. And the reason they are pretending is out of fear—they fear punishment either in this life or in the life to come, if they do not pretend to want, and obey, that which they know in their heart is good. People also pretend out of love—self-love. They like the praise and power that comes from being good, or being perceived as good.

So we are all actors—we act one way, but in our heart, if others could see what is there, they would be very surprised. Little children, who are the greatest in the kingdom of heaven, are not like this. They do not know how to act. Then, as the child grows older, as the poet says, the little actor cons another part—that is, he learns how to be an actor, and pretend.

People who were pretenders, and put on a good outward show but hated the children of God secretly, they went after Jesus. It says in the Bible: "And they watched him, and sent forth spies, which should feign themselves just men, that they might take hold of his words, so they might deliver him unto the power and authority of the governor" (Luke 20:20). How sad to see such blindness, and cruel actions against one who loved them so much!

In the book of Proverbs we read about pretending, lying, dissembling. It is joined with a heart that hates: "He that hateth dissembleth with his lips, and layeth up deceit within him. When he speaketh fair, believe him not, for there are seven abominations in his heart" (Prov 26:24–25). And then it says that this will become known at some point, in the congregation, how matters truly are with the one who is pretending: "[The one whose] hatred is covered by deceit, his wickedness shall be shewed before the whole congregation" (Prov 26:26).

The children of this world are wiser

I AM CONSTANTLY SURPRISED by how seldom people who are Christians are willing to forgive. They, like the heathen in darkness, forgive small slights and little things, usually easily. And they go for years sometimes without anything ever happening to them that is difficult, offensive, or abusive of them. But then when that moment comes, we find out by the fiery trial that this Christian does not want to forgive. For he truly has been wronged. He is in the right, and the other is in the wrong. And the fact that the Christian is in the right and has truly been wronged makes the Christian think that somehow this makes it acceptable not to forgive. He retaliates. He calls the other person evil names as they have done to him. When conversing with other people about the other person, he hints at how bad the person is who abused him. He counter-sues. He never stops to think—this accusation, this slapping, this public shaming, has come to try me, to see what is in my heart. To answer this question: will you forgive even this?

Jesus tried (I often feel, in vain) to teach Christians about this matter of forgiving people who hurt and shame us. Jesus said something enigmatic, something that should make every child of God, every child of the kingdom, every child of light, stop and ponder. Jesus said that "the children of this world are in their generation wiser than the children of light" (Luke 16:8). For if you read the parable about the steward that precedes this statement, you will see that the children of this world, do, in fact, forgive. It is a partial, not a full, forgiveness. That is true. For in the parable, one owed one hundred and the steward forgave fifty of it. The other owed one hundred and the steward forgave eighty of it. So he only partially forgave the debt. But the point is, he did forgive some of it. And, it is also true, as the parable relates, that the child of this world did what he did out of fear and self-love, not because it was the right thing to do. For it says that he did not want to lose his job (Luke 16:3). And he also wanted to keep his friends (Luke 16:4). So he forgave some, but not all, and he forgave for selfish reasons. Nevertheless, this forgiveness was effective in his life. He certainly pleased his lord. And it is likely that he kept friends, and maybe even his high position. We see this in our own jobs and relationships every day. If we let things go, if we forgive, if we forget, if we overlook faults, we are better off.

Christians should not be like this steward, who forgave only partially and for the wrong reasons. Christians should forgive because it is urged by the Holy Spirit in a pure conscience, not because of fear or self-love. And Christians should fully and completely forgive. Indeed, if they do not forgive, they will not be forgiven, as we say in the Lord's Prayer. And Christians should forgive even if it does not benefit them in any way—indeed, even if for some reason it might harm them in a temporal sense.

But a lesson of the parable remains—you are better off if you forgive, whether you are a child of the world or a child of God. Indeed, if we all held grudges nobody would ever talk to anyone. For we all offend.

So then, why don't we forgive? Again, the big offenses, the things that really hurt, that affect our pride, our reputation, why don't we forgive these?

The parable of this steward follows directly after the parable of the prodigal son and his older brother. The older brother could not forgive. So what happened to him in the end? The text gives a grave picture of the state of this older son's heart.

Dearly beloved friends, let us all confess that we are unforgiving, implacable, corner-reapers. Friends,

> Owe no man anything, but to love one another, for he that loveth another hath fulfilled the law. For this, "Thou shalt not commit adultery, thou shalt not kill, thou shalt

not steal, thou shalt not bear false witness, thou shalt not covet;" and if there be any other commandment, it is briefly comprehended in this saying, namely, "Thou shalt love thy neighbor as thyself." Love worketh no will to his neighbor; therefore love is the fulfilling of the law (Rom 13:8–10).

He thinks

TWO OF THE WORST words in the world are "he thinks." Now, at times in the Bible, we get told what people are thinking, but this is rare. However, when we do get told in the Bible what someone was thinking, we can take it as true. But unless we get told from a perfect source what someone else is thinking, then how do we know what another person is thinking?

God "declares unto man what man's thought is" (Amos 4:13). From this text we could even ask—why does a man have to be told by God what that man's thoughts are? Doesn't a man know what his own thoughts are? After all, they are in his own head, his own heart. He is the one thinking them. And yet he needs God to declare his own thoughts to him. So we don't even know what we ourselves think! So how do we, as corrupt humans, know what another person thinks? Or, to use the Hebrew idiom, what another person is speaking in his heart?

Even when the Scripture says, for example, of the heathen, that when they pray, they think they will be heard because of their constant speaking (Matt 6:7)—why do we not be charitable when we look at a heathen and say: I don't know why that heathen is constantly praying and using vain repetitions? Why don't we say: maybe he is searching? Or: maybe he doesn't know any better? For in general, this statement from Scripture is true, that people do use vain repetitions in praying and are not sincere, and they think that they will be heard because of their long speeches. But why are we so sure, in an individual case, with our neighbor, that it applies to our neighbor's thoughts? Couldn't he say the same thing about us? And if he did, how would we feel?

He thinks he is better than me. He thinks he can get away with it. He thinks I am stupid. He thinks he is going to be able to make me jealous. It never ends. Why don't we remember the story about the older brother of the prodigal son? The text says that the younger brother, the prodigal son, went out and wasted his substance in riotous living. But what did the older brother say? He said that the younger brother had spent it all on harlots. So which was it? Riotous living, or harlots? If it was harlots, then how did the older brother know this? And why did he repeat it? And why did he say harlots instead of riotous living? How did he know what the younger brother had been doing in the world? Doesn't it say more about the temptations and lusts of the older brother than it does about the prodigal son? It seems to me the older brother's statement about harlots reveals exactly what he wants to do, but doesn't dare to do out of fear of losing status. Or maybe he does do such things but hides them. Something had gone wrong on the left side in the older brother's heart, and something also was going wrong on the right side: he could not have a mind of compassion and graciousness towards another human, his own brother.

Let us stop assuming the worst—let's assume the best. Let's forgive. "For I know the thoughts that I think towards you, sayeth the Lord, thoughts of peace, and not of evil" (Jer 29:11). All this goodness comes to us from God, even though we have been admonished, and disobeyed these words: "Let none of you imagine evil against his brother in your heart" (Zech 7:10). And God knows how we are. He testifies of us: "Thou sittest and speakest against thy brother; thou slanderest thine own mother's son" (Ps 50:20). And yet God "hath delivered my soul in peace from the battle that was against me" (Ps 55:18).

Shimei

SHIMEI. REMEMBER SHIMEI. THESE words should be constantly on the lips of a Christian. For the words "remember Shimei" summarize the books of 1 and 2 Peter. They say, as Luther was fond of saying to those who had to suffer and be horribly treated: suffer it like a Christian.

Shimei cursed David (2 Sam 16:6). What Shimei said about David, if you attributed the worst motives to David, as many did and do, was true. But if you charitably interpret David's actions, you have compassion on David. Shimei went along and threw mud at David and called out cruel accusations to him. Did David accuse Shimei back? Did he say: what right does he have to say such things? No. He thought Shimei was sent from God to teach him, to teach David. David needed to learn again to be patient, to await the deliverance of God. For he says in the psalms: "My soul, wait only upon God. For my hope is in him" (Ps 62:5).

Always around us are those who, like Joab, urge retaliation. We ourselves feel the lust for revenge in our own flesh. We feel the injustice. We notice that the situation is completely unfair to us. I ask you, was it fair what happened to Jesus? But if you think about it, if Jesus really was an imposter, and not the Son of God, as he testified he was, then those who sentenced him to death did correctly. For that was his crime: blasphemy. He claimed to be a child of God. We claim the same thing, and those in darkness do not believe we speak the truth. But they, like those who sentenced Jesus, do not know any better. That is why they do what they do.

As Jesus cried out, we also should cry out: forgive them, for they do not know what they are doing.

God chose by his unsearchable will to make the captain of our salvation perfect through suffering. The servant is not greater than the master. So, beloved, let us give all diligence and "add to your faith virtue, and to virtue knowledge, and to knowledge temperance, and to temperance patience, and to patience godliness, and to godliness brotherly kindness, and to brotherly kindness charity." For he says to us: "If these things be in you, and abound, they make you that ye shall neither be barren nor unfruitful in the knowledge of our Lord Jesus Christ" (2 Pet 1:5–8).

Love and doctrine

THE WORKING POWER OF faith is love (Gal 5:6). Notice it does not say that the *power* of faith is love, but that the *working power* of faith is love. The energizing power of faith is love. As it says in 1 John 3:14: "We know that we have passed from death unto life, because we love the brethren. He that loveth not his brother abideth in death."

Notice it does not say that the energizing power, or working power, of faith, is doctrine. It is love, not doctrine. Doctrine, correct doctrine (correct teaching), always comes to a converted heart, along with love. It always comes. But it is not the working power there in that converted heart. Love is. Truth never converted anyone. Only grace did. Truth convicts when it is preached to those outside of God's kingdom. And inside God's kingdom truth gently admonishes, rebukes, and comforts. True doctrine does not change stony hearts into hearts of flesh. When doctrine effects, it does so by the working power of love and grace. Love. Not fear or any other thing. It is written: "He that feareth is not made perfect in love" (1 John 4:18). And: "Hereby perceive we the love of God, because he laid down his life for us. And we ought to lay down our lives for the brethren" (1 John 3:16).

Grace teaches. Why does Peter say "above all things have fervent charity among yourselves; for charity shall cover a multitude of sins" (1 Pet 4:8)? Notice he says "above all," and he doesn't say, above all things have correct doctrine among yourselves. For if there is charity and abundant overflowing forgiveness, this will melt hearts and bring about understanding of doctrine better than any other working power.

As he says: "Seeing ye have purified your souls in obeying the truth through the Spirit unto unfeigned love of the brethren, see that ye love one another with a pure heart fervently" (1 Pet 1:22). And if you understand all mysteries, even mysteries of doctrine, but lack love, you are nothing (1 Cor 13:2). All the correct doctrine in the world will not help you if you lack love.

How many of us have not gone out visiting other children of God with whom we have differences, even deep differences of doctrinal understandings? Even of Scripture? We all have. And what have we remembered? What has convinced us we have been in the wrong? All the explanations, all the quotations, all the orations and displays of the powers of the mind? No. It has been the smile of the little child. It has been the sincerity of heart of the others. It has been the forgiveness of sins that was preached. It has been the gentle reminder from Scriptures. It has been the friendly words said to us as we had coffee and donuts. It was the offer to come help us out with the moving project. It was the agreement to remember a troubled youth. These acts and words of love melted our hearts so that we even said on our way home: my goodness, I do believe I understand now what that person was trying to explain to me about doctrinal matters. It is clear.

A tender heart, a loved and melted soul, a pure conscience—these take hold of and understand correct doctrine easily, like a child. It is written: "And the Lord make you to increase and abound in love one toward another, and toward all men, even as we do toward you" (1 Thess 3:12).

The goal of the commandment, the fulfillment of the commandment, and the end of the commandment, is charity out of a pure heart and of a good conscience, and faith that is not faked (1 Tim 1:5). This is what Paul first and foremost writes to Timothy. After reminding Timothy to love, Paul goes on to other topics. So it is only after he has reminded Timothy about faith and a tender heart that Paul goes on to delve into doctrinal issues, which are truly also important.

Let us dress ourselves with charity above all things. As it is written: "Forbearing one another, and forgiving one another, if any man have a quarrel against any, even as Christ forgave you, so also do you. And above all these things put on charity, which is the bond of perfectness" (Col 3:13–14).

Note that man

IT SAYS IN THE Bible in one place: "And if any man obey not our word by this epistle, note that man, and have no company with him, that he may be ashamed" (2 Thess 3:14). In other words, if someone is disobeying the Word of God, we are to note who they are. The words "and have no company with him," would be better translated to the effect, "and don't get mixed up with him." The goal, as the text says, is that the person who is disobedience would feel shame over sin, over disobedience, and repent. As the next verse says: "Yet count him not as an enemy, but admonish him as a brother" (2 Thess 3:15).

Now I would ask you a question about this text. How do you know that someone is disobeying the Word of God? Because this is the decisive factor in applying this text into our own lives. For example, what if we see someone who seems to be struggling? Who may, on the one hand, look like he is disobeying the Word of God, but who might not be? How do we know?

First, we look at the commandments. There we see exactly what sin is (Exod 20, Deut 5, Job 31). Now if, as happened in Corinth (1 Cor 5—6), the person is openly breaking the commandments, everyone knows it. Thus, we do know, we know perfectly well, that the person is disobeying the Word of God. Indeed, if the situation is as it was in Corinth, everyone knows. But, in most situations, I submit to you, it is not clear. In other words, there is the question of motives. There is the question of interpretation of actions or words.

If we are not sure that someone is disobeying the Word of God, then this text from Thessalonians does not apply. If the person seems to be struggling, or seems to be disobedient, we are commanded to go help him, as the Good Samaritan did. We are commanded to visit those in prison, to reach out to the hungry. As it says in Isaiah 58, we are to "loose the bands of wickedness, to undo the heavy burdens, to let the oppressed go free, and break every yoke." We are to deal our bread to the hungry, and bring the poor who are cast out into our own house. When we see the naked, we are to cover him, and we are not to hide ourselves from our own flesh.

Be careful, my friends, not to avoid people because of an assumption. Be careful not to "not keep company with" someone because of an assumption or a rumor, or the testimony of some seemingly important person. It says: "Now I beseech you, brethren, mark them which cause divisions and offenses contrary to the doctrine which ye have learned; and avoid them" (Rom 16:17). And as for the man in Corinth, it was said of him: "Put away from among you that wicked person" (1 Cor 5:13). But we are not to avoid anyone, or put away anyone, or stop keeping company with anyone, unless God has made it very clear to us that the person is in wickedness and is unrepentant about it. God will cleave the earth and swallow them up so we know how matters really are as God did with Korah and Korah's followers. But if we judge for ourselves, and decide wrongly, we break the eighth commandment by slandering someone, and by not interpreting their speech and words in the best possible light. Then we are in great danger. What if it is decided of us: "Thou hast not given water to the weary to drink; and thou hast withholden bread from the hungry" (Job 22:7)? Shouldn't it better be said of us, as it is of Christ: "He hath dispersed, he hath given to the poor" (Ps 112:9)? For we are told that if our enemy is hungry we are to "give him bread to eat; and if he be thirsty, give him water to drink" (Prov 25:21). And: "He that giveth unto the poor shall not lack, but he that hideth his eyes shall have many a curse" (Prov 28:27). We should be sober, and not think of ourselves as more highly than we ought (Rom 12:3), but rather, judge this, that we ourselves could easily fall. "Be not overcome of evil, but overcome evil with good" (Rom 12:21).

Jesus says: "For I was an hungred, and ye gave me meat: I was thirsty, and ye gave me drink. I was a stranger, and ye took me in; naked, and ye clothed me. I was sick, and ye visited me. I was in prison, and ye came unto me" (Matt 25:35–36). So let us be sure that we do not assume someone isn't hungry, and thirsty, and a stranger, and sick, and in prison, until we know they are not. Otherwise, we ourselves will be shown to be blind, and our fate will be that of the angel of the church, unto whom Jesus said: "Because thou sayest, I am rich, and increased with goods, and have need of nothing; and knowest not that thou art wretched, and miserable, and poor, and blind, and naked" (Rev 3:17).

It is written: "Thou shalt not see thy brother's ass or his ox fall down by the way, and hide thyself from them. Thou shalt surely help him lift them up again" (Deut 22:4). The same is also said of our enemy's livestock (Exod 23:4). We do not wish to end up like an Ammonite or a Moabite who "shall not enter into the congregation of the Lord forever" for this sin: "They met you not with bread and with water in the way, when ye came forth out of Egypt" (Deut 23:3–4). For if we afflict the downtrodden it shall go poorly with us, as it is written: "If thou afflict them in any wise, and they cry at all unto me, I will surely hear their cry; and my wrath shall wax hot, and I will kill you with the sword, and your wives shall be widows, and your children fatherless" (Exod 22:23–24). Or, dear friend, do you not remember the words of the brothers, when they realized what they had done to Joseph: "And they said one to another, 'We are verily guilty concerning our brother, in that we saw the anguish of his soul, when he besought us, and we would not hear, and that is why this distress has come upon us'" (Gen 42:21)?

Only us

THE CHILDREN OF GOD do not claim that all those who do not believe as they do are under condemnation. God does. God says that all those who do not hold in their hearts the same faith that the children of God hold in their hearts are under condemnation and wrath. "Tribulation and anguish, upon every soul of man that doeth evil, of the Jew first, and also of the Gentile" (Rom 2:9).

The children of God do not believe that all those who are not children of God are for sure at some time in the future going to hell. They can only say at a certain given moment in time, to someone who is a child of the world, that if that person died at that moment that person would be judged as a child of wrath. As it is written: "Behold, all souls are mine; as the soul of the father, so also the soul of the son is mine. The soul that sinneth, it shall die" (Ezek 18:4). For the children of God are not God. And therefore they do not know if the child of the world they are speaking with is ever going to receive the grace of repentance or not. And they also do not know if they themselves will be preserved in the grace of God until their last breath. Thus, the information the child of God gives to a child of the world about their destination is only for that moment. It is for today. It is written: "Today, if ye will hear his voice, harden not your hearts" (Ps 95:7). And it is also written: "The Lord made not this covenant with our fathers, but with us, even us, who are all of us here alive this day" (Deut 5:3). Tomorrow the situation could be completely different. And nobody knows that except God.

The children of God also very definitely do not say that all those who are not part of the earthly organizations that the children of God have organized are under condemnation, are children of hell and death. That is completely contrary to Scripture. All the little children on this earth, millions of them, are children of God, whether baptized or not, whether they have ever heard of Jesus or not. For all human beings conceived have the Holy Spirit at conception. Children, as they grow, can lose this Holy Spirit by the hardening of their hearts through sin, but we preach to all people, as the prophets did, to return to God. That is, to return, to return to your childhood faith. See Isaiah 21:12, 44:22, 55:7, Jeremiah 3:22, 36:6, Ezekiel 18:23, and Malachi 3:7, for example.

All earthly organizations that the children of God set up are simply that: earthly. They come and go, and change and shift. Sometimes an earthly organization that the children of God set up becomes swallowed up by the world. That is, all the people who are in it are lost to the world through the deceitfulness of sin. When there is not one person left with the Spirit of God, all is lost. But if there is one, a messenger, an interpreter, then matters can go well:

> If there be a messenger with him, an interpreter, one among a thousand, to shew unto man his uprightness. Then he is gracious unto him, and saith, "Deliver him from going down to the pit; I have found a ransom." His flesh shall be fresher than a child's. He shall return to the days of his youth. He shall pray unto God, and he will be favorable unto him, and he shall see his face with joy; for he will render unto man his righteousness. He looketh upon men, and if any say, "I have sinned, and perverted that which was right, and it profited me not . . . " (Job 33:23–27).

Among the gods

"AMONG THE GODS THERE is none like unto thee, O Lord" (Ps 86:8). Why does the Bible mention other gods? One place to look for an answer is in the *Large Catechism*. In the meaning of the first commandment in the *Large Catechism* it is explained that all men worship gods. So there are many gods, in a sense. Because to have a god is to love something, and to want it and respect it. All men love and want and respect something. Therefore all men have a god or gods. It is true that people call themselves atheists, but in essence they are not atheists; they simply worship other gods. For they want and love something. Whatever they want and love and fear the loss of the most, the very most, is their highest god. For most people it is mammon or pleasure or power.

So the Bible mentions these other gods, so that we would know that it is possible to be in the power of another god besides the Living God. For the one to whom you yield yourself a slave to obey, you are his slave (Rom 6:16). We have a tendency to worship ourselves as gods as well, for the serpent tempts, promising "ye shall be as gods" (Gen 3:5). We want to love and obey ourselves, our own minds, instead of God's mind.

There are other gods, but they are "strange gods" (Gen 35:2-4). They are the "gods of Egypt" (Exod 12:12). They are made with hands and will perish (Acts 19:26). They are by nature, not gods (Gal 4:8). They are worshipped, admired, respected. People serve them, hope for good from them, and fear the loss of them above all things.

We do have other gods we serve besides the Living God, in the sense that we love our families and serve them, or we serve the leaders (Exod 22:28), or we work for money. But we are not enslaved by our love for these things, if our heart is right. They are not our highest god: "Thou shalt have no other gods before me" (Exod 20:3). For we know that "there is none other God but one. For though there be such that are called gods, whether in heaven or in earth, (as there be gods many, and lords many,) but to us there is but one God, the Father" (1 Cor 8:4–6).

God is the one who saves. The songwriter asks: "Who is like unto thee, O Lord, among the gods? Who is like thee, glorious in holiness, fearful in praises, doing wonders?" (Exod 15:11). The living God is above all other gods in power, as it is testified: "Now I know that the Lord is greater than all gods" (Exod 18:11).

Preaching from envy and strife

I LOVE WHEN MINISTERS take the first chapter of Philippians as a text and have to read verses 15-17: "Some indeed preach Christ even of envy and strife, and some also of good will. The one preach Christ of contention, not sincerely, supposing to add affliction to my bonds. But the other of love, knowing that I am set for the defence [argument] of the gospel." Ministers never deal with this part—they skip right by. But this text is there for a reason. It is to teach us to wonder about ourselves, to make us ask: am I preaching out of envy and strife?

For we all get confused at times. What does it say about the state of our soul when we are confused, or not understanding something about faith? To answer this question, let me ask you, when Paul accused Peter to his face "because he was to be blamed" (Gal 2:11), if Peter would have died in that moment, where would his soul have gone? In the moment when the disciples asked Jesus in the first chapter of Acts, "Lord, wilt thou at this time restore again the kingdom to Israel?" (1:6), thinking of him in a very earthly way, where were the disciples—in what kingdom? For a tree is known by its fruits and by the confession of the lips the contents of the heart are known.

When Philip asked Jesus in John: "Lord, shew us the Father, and it sufficeth us" (14:8), what did Jesus answer? What do you think Jesus thought about the condition of Philip's heart at that time? What about when the disciples questioned him about why he went up to Jerusalem? For in one place when Jesus taught of the way of the cross, Peter said: "Be it far from thee, Lord, this shall not be unto thee" (Matt 16:22). Jesus even called Peter "Satan," because Jesus was so opposed to the doctrine Peter taught then. Indeed, the matter was hidden from the disciples (Luke 18:34). What about when the disciples argued about who was the greatest? Was that not very bad doctrine and understanding that the disciples had at that time? And we know that "that which beareth thorns and briers is rejected, and is nigh unto cursing; whose end is to be burned" (Heb 6:8). So we notice in Scripture that believers can understand doctrine wrongly.

Let's go back to the start of the letter to the Philippians. When a person is in a wrong understanding of doctrine, or is preaching with a really bad purpose, does this mean that he has lost the Holy Spirit? Is it right to tell that person he is in a wrong spirit? No. It is not kind to make that judgment rashly about another. For it is written: "In his love and in his pity he redeemed them; and he bare them, and carried them all the days of old" (Isa 63:9). And: "For with what judgment ye judge, ye shall be judged; and with what measure ye mete, it shall be measured to you again" (Matt 7:2). We should be very careful and gentle and patient with those who are erring or misunderstanding (Rom 15:2).

For what is said of all the children of God? That we are all always erring, always:

> For their heart was not right with him, neither were they steadfast in his covenant. But he, being full of compassion, forgave their iniquity, and destroyed them not. Yea, many a time turned he his anger away, and did not stir up all his wrath. For he remembered that they were but flesh; a wind that passeth away, and cometh not again (Ps 78:37–39).

And Moses tells us to understand this of ourselves: "Ye have been rebellious against the Lord from the day that I knew you" (Deut 9:24).

The heart of a child of God confesses his wickedness and God's immeasurable mercy:

> We have sinned with our fathers, we have committed iniquity, we have done wickedly. Our fathers understood

> not thy wonders in Egypt; they remembered not the multitude of thy mercies; but provoked him at the sea, even at the Red Sea. Nevertheless he saved them for his name's sake, that he might make his mighty power to be known (Ps 106:6–8).

It is faith of the heart that saves. And we are to be "apt to teach" (1 Tim 3:2, 2 Tim 2:24), to help each other, and we are to be as gentle as Jesus was with Philip in doing so (1 Cor 13:1–4). Sometimes it is necessary to say of someone's doctrine: "Get thee behind me Satan" (Matt 16:23), but even this we can exhort in love. We should be upset with ourselves when we see error in ourselves, but God will help us be corrected in his time through the Spirit in the congregation and by his Word (Deut 21:1–9).

What if we are being tried? What if that which is false is being brought among us for another reason? That is, to try us, to test us? As it is written:

> If there arise among you a prophet, or a dreamer of dreams, and giveth thee a sign or a wonder, and the sign or the wonder come to pass, whereof he spake unto thee, saying, "Let us go after other gods, which thou hast not known, and let us serve them"; thou shalt not hearken unto the words of that prophet, or that dreamer of dreams; for the Lord your God proveth you, to know whether ye love the Lord your God with all your heart and with all your soul (Deut 13:1–3).

Death is swallowed up in victory

PEOPLE WHO CONSIDER THE first death, or being enslaved or imprisoned in the body, as worse than the second death, or slavery to sin, cannot understand much of what God sets forth for us in the Bible. Peter says in Acts 2:29 about David: "He is both dead and buried, and his sepulchre is with us unto this day." In other words, David is certainly dead. But David also sings: "I shall not die, but live" (Ps 118:17). And: "For thou wilt not leave my soul in hell" (Ps 16:10). And David testifies that he will live forever: "O Lord my God, I will give thanks unto thee for ever" (Ps 30:12).

David did not die the second death, only the first death. For it is written: "He that overcometh shall not be hurt of the second death" (Rev 2:11). Death had no power over David. It is written: "Blessed and holy is he that hath part in the first resurrection; on such the second death hath no power" (Rev 20:6).

But we have already many times heard about the picture "death" and how it is used to warn us, exhort us, and comfort us in the Bible. To kill, in the Bible, as Luther was fond of explaining, often means to proclaim eternal death to someone who abides in death. Indeed, David asks for this very thing for himself (1 Sam 20:8).

Let's look at another picture-image. Jesus says: "Whatsoever you shall bind on earth shall be bound in heaven and whatsoever ye shall loose on earth shall be loosed in heaven" (Matt 18:18). To be bound is a picture used in the Bible to teach us about the truths of the soul. A parallel verse uses a different verb: "Whose soever sins ye remit, they are remitted unto them; and whose soever sins ye retain, they are retained" (John 20:23).

Being bound is exactly the same as being dead. It is the same as being spiritually enslaved, as not having your sins remitted. Different pictures in the Bible are used to teach the same thing—being bound is a state of the heart. For example, Uzziah was bound in his sin, by God, and the picture used is one of leprosy:

> But when he was strong his heart was lifted up to his destruction. For he transgressed against the Lord his God, and went into the temple of the Lord to burn incense upon the altar of incense. And Azariah the priest went in after him, and with him fourscore priests of the Lord, that were valiant men. And they withstood Uzziah the king, and said unto him, "It appertaineth not to thee, Uzziah, to burn incense unto the Lord, but to the priests the sons of Aaron, that are consecrated to burn incense. Go out of the sanctuary, for thou hast trespassed; neither shall it be for thine honor from the Lord God." Then Uzziah was wroth, and had a censer in his hand to burn incense. And while he was wroth with the priests, the leprosy even rose up in his forehead before the priests in the house of the Lord, from beside the incense altar. And Azariah the chief priest, and all the priests, looked upon him, and, behold, he was leprous in his forehead, and they thrust him out from thence; yea, he himself hasted also to go out, because the Lord had smitten him (2 Chr 26:16–20).

Just as I, a child of God, do not bind anyone by my own power and my own word, so also I, as a child of God, do not kill anyone by my own power and my own word. I only declare someone to be bound or dead according to the Holy Spirit. God says: "I kill, and I make alive; I wound, and I heal; neither is there any that can deliver out of my hand" (Deut 32:39). So it is not us, but God. We only deliver a message. "The Lord killeth, and maketh alive; he bringeth down to the grave, and bringeth up" (1 Sam 2:6). It says in Job: "For he maketh sore, and bindeth up; he woundeth, and his hands make whole" (5:18). So we exhort: "Come, and let us return unto the

Lord; for he hath torn, and he will heal us; he hath smitten, and he will bind us up" (Hos 6:1). We do not kill, or tear, or smite, or bind, of ourselves. We have no power to do so. As it is written: "These things saith he that is holy, he that is true, he that hath the key of David, he that openeth, and no man shutteth; and shutteth, and no man openeth" (Rev 3:7). But, as a child of God, I do declare, or teach, that someone is bound, or is in death, or is in slavery to sin. This I do all the time. For I am commanded "to deliver such an one unto Satan for the destruction of the flesh, that the spirit may be saved in the day of the Lord Jesus" (1 Cor 5:5). And again: "If there come any unto you, and bring not this doctrine, receive him not into your house, neither bid him God speed; for he that biddeth him God speed is partaker of his evil deeds" (2 John 1:10–11). Paul proclaimed these truths to Hymenaeus and Alexander. Of them he testified: "I have delivered unto Satan, that they may learn not to blaspheme" (1 Tim 1:20).

The congregation of God on earth, which has the Word of God, preaches. The Holy Spirit does the work. It is written: "He that believeth on him is not condemned, but he that believeth not is condemned already" (John 3:18). The Word of God separates the clean from the unclean. The priests "shall teach my people the difference between the holy and profane, and cause them to discern between the unclean and the clean" (Ezek 44:23). The Word of God convicts or heals consciences. As it says in John 8:9, some were "convicted by their own conscience," and so they left. When we know for certain someone is bound in their sins, or dead in them, slaves of hell, we declare that to them. Then they know their condition. Paul writes that he would not have known his condition unless the Word had come to him and informed him (Rom 7:9).

In the congregation of God, we, the living, have made a promise by the Spirit to remind the others that if they fall from faith, they abide in death, and are children of wrath; as it is written: "And they entered into a covenant to seek the Lord God of their fathers with all their heart and with all their soul, that whosoever would not seek the Lord God of Israel should be put to death, whether small or great, whether man or woman" (2 Chr 15:12–13). I, as an individual child of God, should be the first one to go pull someone out of a matter of death if I am the first or only one to see it. But if they do not hear me, I should bring it to the congregation (Deut 13:9, Matthew 18:17).

So we preach. We say to the dead: "Arise" (Isa 60:1, Luke 8:54). As it is written: "Awake thou that sleepest, and arise from the dead, and Christ shall give thee light" (Eph 5:14). We say to the sleeping and dumb: "Awake and sing" (Isa 26:19). We say to the barren: "More are the children of the desolate than the children of the married wife" (Isa 54:1). We say to the blind: "See" (Isa 42:18). And we say to the bound and sick: "Be loosed" (Luke 13:12). We don't know what kind of heart the Word we teach will fall on. It has nothing to do with us. But God says, and we repeat: "Seek ye the Lord while he may be found, call ye upon him while he is near" (Isa 55:6). And: "Seek him that maketh the seven stars and Orion, and turneth the shadow of death into the morning, and maketh the day dark with night, that calleth for the waters of the sea, and poureth them out upon the face of the earth. The Lord is his name" (Amos 5:8).

If God stops calling, stops offering, there is no hope for that person unto whom the door is closed. God does warn us: "My Spirit will not always dispute" (Gen 6:3). But we don't know who this has happened to. We don't know who God has ended hope for. Jesus knew that Judas's day of calling was over. For Jesus was God. But we, like the disciples, do not know. And what did Jesus do for Judas, even knowing the condition of his heart? He forgave him. He washed his feet (John 13:12–14). Sadly, it had no effect. But Jesus did do this act of love to Judas.

In Amos it is written that God can take his Word away. He can cause it to no longer be heard:

> Behold, the days come, saith the Lord God, that I will send a famine in the land, not a famine of bread, nor a thirst for water, but of hearing the words of the Lord. And they shall wander from sea to sea, and from the north even to the east, they shall run to and fro to seek the word of the Lord, and shall not find it (8:11–12).

So it happened with Edom (Obad 1:10–14). Other examples of the end of a time of visitation of the Word are plentiful. One is Eli. God told him that forgiveness preached to him would no longer have any effect:

> For I have told him that I will judge his house forever for the iniquity which he knoweth; because his sons made themselves accursed, and he restrained them not. And therefore I have sworn unto the house of Eli, that the iniquity of Eli's house shall not be atoned for with sacrifice nor offering forever (1 Sam 3:13–14).

So the end of Eli was exceedingly sad.

But I want to end with this. What did some of the saints do when they knew, because God had told them, that the end of the time of visitation had come for someone, or for some nation? David knew that Saul was lost. Nevertheless he prayed for him and loved his enemies (Ps 35:13). He even declared that whoever finally killed Saul is an Amalek, of the devil (2 Sam 1:11–16). And what about Moses? He says that he would wish himself in hell and death in place of the people who have sinned (Exod 32:31–33). It is written:

> And Moses returned unto the Lord, and said, "Oh, this people have sinned a great sin, and have made them gods of gold. Yet now, if thou wilt forgive their sin—; and if not, blot me, I pray thee, out of thy book which thou hast written." And the Lord said unto Moses, "Whosoever hath sinned against me, him will I blot out of my book."

And David says the same of Absalom: "O my son Absalom, my son, my son Absalom! would God I had died for thee, O Absalom, my son, my son!" (2 Sam 18:33). What about the Jews? They lost their day of visitation, and everyone knew it and knows it. But what does Paul, knowing, or suspecting this, say? He prays for them, just like Moses. He wishes to trade places with them (Rom 9:3).

We don't know what God is doing in the hearts of men. We can only go by what they confess to us. If they confess that they are not in faith, we don't greet them. But if God gives them a remorseful heart, we forgive. And as the catechism says, we should forgive in the name of the Father, Son, and Holy Ghost, and then add a few Bible verses to the penitent one for their encouragement and learning. We don't just proclaim forgiveness. We also encourage the person who is forgiven with comforting and reminding words from Scripture. It is good to know the Bible for these occasions.

God knows the hearts of men (Acts 1:24). We do not err in forgiving. We err in calling that which is darkness light. We err when we tell someone who we know abides in the kingdom of Satan that he abides in Christ. He does not, and we ought to tell him the truth (Isa 5:20). But we do not err in forgiving, no matter how convoluted or odd the confession or request for forgiveness. Our words may fall on barren ground, but only God knows that. And he also knows if later on that seed will germinate and bear fruit.

Choice

BEFORE SAUL FELL FROM faith it was told to him: "And the Spirit of the Lord will come upon thee, and thou shalt prophesy with them, and shalt be turned into another man" (1 Sam 10:6). And it says that "God gave [Saul] another heart" (1 Sam 10:9). God can, by his Spirit, give another heart to a person. He can take out a stony heart and put in a heart of flesh. But the person cannot choose to have this happen. It is God's choice, and the operation of the Spirit. "Ye have not chosen me, but I have chosen you" (John 15:16). God chooses of free grace (Deut 7:7).

It is true that we are commanded to "choose life" (Deut 30:19), but this is a command. It does not say: you are able to choose life. It is a command. It says: choose life, just as Cain was commanded: rule over sin. We are not able to rule over sin of ourselves. We are not able to choose life of ourselves. God operates in us and gives us a heart to choose life. It is written:

> And I will give them one heart, and I will put a new spirit within you; and I will take the stony heart out of their flesh, and will give them a heart of flesh, that they may walk in my statutes, and keep mine ordinances, and do them, and they shall be my people, and I will be their God. But as for them whose heart walketh after their abominations, I will recompense their way upon their own heads, said the Lord God (Ezek 11:19–21).

You notice the emphasis here is not on our ability to choose, but on God giving a heart, of God putting a changed mind into a person. As it is written: "And I will give them a heart to know me, that I am the Lord, and they shall be my people, and I will be their God, for they shall return unto me with their whole heart" (Jer 24:7). And the prayer is: "Let [God] not leave us, nor forsake us, that he may incline our hearts unto him, to walk in all his ways, and to keep his commandments, and his statutes, and his judgments, which he commanded our fathers" (1 Kgs 8:57–58).

Notice that the first step is God doing his work in the heart. After God does his work in the heart, then the obedience to him follows. Elijah prayed: "Hear me, O Lord, hear me, that this people may know that thou art the Lord God, and that thou hast turned their heart back again" (1 Kgs 18:37).

Oxen

ONE OF THE BEST passages of Scripture to memorize, if you want to understand Scripture better, is 1 Corinthians 9:9. It reads: "For it is written in the law of Moses: 'Thou shalt not muzzle the mouth of the ox that treadeth out the corn.' Doth God take care for oxen?" Let us consider this text carefully. Paul read the books of Moses. He saw this passage: "Thou shalt not muzzle the ox when he treadeth out the corn" (Deut 25:4). Did Paul, on reading this, think: "Oh, wonderful, now I know how I, being commanded by God in the law of Moses, ought to treat my oxen." Or did Paul, on reading this, think: "Oh, now I know what the law of Moses legislated about how to care about oxen way back a long time ago." No. Paul did not think either of these things. He thought the text was not about oxen. He thought the text was about preachers and preaching.

Look carefully at his words: "Doth God take care for oxen?" Paul is actually purposefully refuting anyone who thinks this text from Moses is about terrestrial things, about carnal things, about how the laws of earth and man are structured. For he goes on: "Or saith he it altogether for our sakes? For our sakes, no doubt, this is written: that he that ploweth should plow in hope; and that he that thresheth in hope should be partaker of his hope" (1 Cor 9:10).

Keep this text in mind when you are reading Moses. If you consider Moses as one who minds earthly things you will not understand what Moses is trying to teach. For Paul in another place even repeats this claim, that the laws in Moses are about the matters of God's house: "For the Scripture saith: 'Thou shalt not muzzle the ox that treadeth out the corn.' And: 'The laborer is worthy of his reward'" (1 Tim 5:18).

The hardening of Pharaoh's heart

THERE COMES A TIME of visitation to a man, as there did to Pharaoh. But when the time of visitation is over, when the door to God is closed, there is no hope for that person any longer. For it is written: "And the key of the house of David will I lay upon his shoulder; so he shall open, and none shall shut; and he shall shut, and none shall open" (Isa 22:22). And again: "These things saith he that is holy, he that is true, he that hath the key of David, he that openeth, and no man shutteth; and shutteth, and no man openeth" (Rev 3:7). Sometimes a place is given a time of visitation, and then the candlestick is removed from that place (Jer 7:12). But most familiar to all of us is the truth that God gives a time of visitation to each man individually.

God had set before Pharaoh an open door, but Pharaoh turned away. God showed him signs and wonders, but Pharaoh did not take heed. It is written: "He, that being often reproved hardeneth his neck, shall suddenly be destroyed, and that without remedy" (Prov 29:1).

God calls and rebukes for a very long time, but his patience will not be forever. He testifies to us that he has called and we have refused: "I have stretched out my hand, and no man regarded. But ye have set at nought all my counsel, and would none of my reproof; I also will laugh at your calamity; I will mock when your fear cometh" (Prov 1:24–26). As it is written:

> And the Lord God of their fathers sent to them by his messengers, rising up betimes, and sending; because he had compassion on his people, and on his dwelling place.

> But they mocked the messengers of God, and despised his words, and misused his prophets, until the wrath of the Lord arose against his people, till there was no remedy (2 Chr 36:15–16).

And:

> But they refused to hearken, and pulled away the shoulder, and stopped their ears, that they should not hear. Yea, they made their hearts as an adamant stone, lest they should hear the law, and the words which the Lord of hosts hath sent in his spirit by the former prophets; therefore came a great wrath from the Lord of hosts (Zech 7:11–12).

So our times are in God's hands, and we ought to listen and hear him when he calls.

So it happened for Pharaoh. God sent his Word to Pharaoh for a long time. Eventually God no longer called. It was not that there was not forgiveness for Pharaoh, it was that Pharaoh did not want it, except as a fake-forgiveness, and a cloak for sin. He had committed the sin that Esau committed, the sin of blasphemy against the Holy Ghost. For this, there is not forgiveness (Matt 12:31). Esau had fallen outside of the kingdom of God. There is no forgiveness outside of the kingdom of God. There is forgiveness only inside the fortress of grace, just as Moses writes:

> At the end of every seven years thou shalt make a release. And this is the manner of the release: every creditor that lendeth ought unto his neighbor shall release it; he shall not exact it of his neighbor, or of his brother; because it is called the Lord's release. Of a foreigner thou mayest exact it again; but that which is thine with thy brother thine hand shall release (Deut 15:1–3).

A person can be in such a condition that he no longer asks, or knows to ask for help, because his heart has been hardened. Because those who are in that condition do not know their condition. They think things are well for them. So it is for heretics. So it was for Pharaoh. The living Word reminds them that they abide in their sin (Lev 19:17), it demands repayment of every debt, an accounting of every sin, so that they realize their lost condition and run to Christ's wounds for mercy (Gal 3:24).

Esau was like Pharaoh. Esau did not find a place of forgiveness, because his day of visitation had gone past. God had closed the door: "For ye know how that afterward, when he would have inherited the blessing, he was rejected. For he found no place of repentance, though he sought it carefully with tears" (Heb 12:17). Notice that it does not say Esau did not find a place of forgiveness, it says that Esau did not find a place of repentance. That place of repentance is that open door that only God can give. And God can also remove it, as he did to Joab (1 Kgs 2:28–34). It is written:

> Strive to enter in at the strait gate; for many, I say unto you, will seek to enter in, and shall not be able. When once the master of the house is risen up, and hath shut to the door, and ye begin to stand outside, and to knock at the door, saying, "Lord, Lord, open unto us;" and he shall answer and say unto you, "I know you not whence ye are" (Luke 13:24–25).

Also:

> For it is impossible for those who were once enlightened, and have tasted of the heavenly gift, and were made partakers of the Holy Ghost, and have tasted the good word of God, and the powers of the world to come, if they shall fall away, to renew them again unto repentance; seeing they crucify to themselves the Son of God afresh, and put him to an open shame (Heb 6:4–6).

And it is also written that if we sin smugly, or presumptuously, or willfully, after we have received knowledge of the truth "there remaineth no more sacrifice for sins, but a certain fearful looking for of judgment and fiery indignation, which shall devour the adversaries" (Heb 10:26–27).

It is not in our hands. It is written that the Scripture said to Pharoah: "Even for this same purpose have I raised thee up, that I might shew my power in thee, and that my name might be declared throughout all the earth." And then it concludes: "Therefore hath he mercy on whom he will have mercy, and whom he will he hardeneth" (Rom 9:17–18). We ought to take comfort in this truth: it is in God's hands. It is written: "Moreover whom he did predestinate, them he also called; and whom he called, them he also justified; and whom he justified, them he also glorified" (Rom 8:30). Also: "But as many as received him, to them gave he power to become the sons of God, even to them that believe on his name" (John 1:12). For God has been merciful to us, to sinners: "According as he hath chosen us in him before the foundation of the world, that we should be holy and without blame before him in love." For God has predestinated us "unto the adoption of children by Jesus Christ to himself, according to the good pleasure of his will" (Eph 1:4–5).

Probably Pharaoh would not forgive. And this is why he was not forgiven. For he who does not forgive his neighbor, from the heart, his trespasses, will not be forgiven (Matt 18:35). For God commands us to blessing (Ps 133:3). Of Christ it is said: "He asked life of thee, and thou gavest it him, even length of days for ever and ever" (Ps 21:4). And all that he has he has given to us, for we are Christ's and Christ is God's (1 Cor 3:23).

The altar and the lamb

THEOLOGY USES METAPHORS. DOING word-work to a modern world means reorganizing new words to apply to ancient concepts. One uses the same metaphors over and over, which are from the Scripture: death/life, marriage/man/woman, sickness/health (which includes leprosy), nature (which includes vines and planting/harvest), seeing/blind, slave/free, law-court/judgment, naked/clothed, food/eating/starving, family.

Now if you take away the above-listed metaphors, you are left with almost nothing of Scripture. You can almost throw away the entire book once you throw out the possibilities of using the above picture-images from daily human life to try to explain the spiritual, the invisible.

Two great exceptions come to mind. If I go through the Bible in my mind and see images from daily life being used to describe the spiritual, there are two that are not universally known and easily comprehensible to anyone, regardless of his culture and regardless of whether or not he has ever read the Bible before or heard of anything that is in it. These are the altar and the lamb. I think I am not wrong in saying these are the only two major images of wide usage in the Bible that are "manufactured," or not taken from nature and from commonly known items of daily human life. There are images that are not often used in the Bible, such as a dish, or a ball, but even these are easily recognizable to all people, regardless of background or culture. People know what a dish is, and washing: "I will wipe Jerusalem as a man wipeth a dish, wiping it, and turning it upside down" (2 Kgs 21:13). All children throw balls:

"He will surely violently turn and toss thee like a ball into a large country" (Isa 22:18).

Jesus made up parables, or allegories, if you prefer that term. But they all fit into the categories I mentioned in the first paragraph: night/day (part of nature), planting/harvest, sickness/health, etc. Both Paul and the writer of the book of Hebrews use building or body pictures, planting and harvest pictures, eating images. Again, all of these are familiar to any human being; just because he is a human he knows at least the picture from nature, if not the invisible realm of truth to which it points. For we all eat. We all have a body. We all know what a brother is. We all know what plants are. But this is not true of the altar and the lamb. These are not immediately familiar or obvious to people. The application to a spiritual lesson is thus not immediately obvious. It has to be explained. What I find so striking about this though, is that the altar/sacrifice/lamb/goat image starts right away in Genesis 3 after the fall into sin. It goes on in the next chapter in the story of Cain and Abel. It shows up in Noah, and the stories of the patriarchs. Moses adds an elaborate worship service to it, and David adds a temple. A good portion of the book of Hebrews is devoted to explaining the entire elaborate arrangement.

What is there to conclude from this? Read the Bible. As we can't lose the language, we also can't lose the images. We can't replace them. Luther, in arguing about the Trinity, took issue with the word "trinity" itself. Why? Because it is not a word that appears in Scripture. Following Luther, we should use the word, but we should be wary of the word. Should we popularize a word or phrase or image that is not in Scripture when we have perfectly useful words and images in Scripture?

Dear child, have a care. In one presentation I saw recently, the presenter pointed out that we always say to "be a light unto the world." But he cautioned us, and reminded us what Scripture says: "Ye are the light of the world" (Matt 5:14). There is a world of difference between "unto" and "of."

God will help us in these things. It is written: "Write the vision, and make it plain upon tables, that he may run that readeth it" (Hab 2:2). And: "Blessed is he that readeth, and they that hear the words of this prophecy, and keep those things which are written therein; for the time is at hand" (Rev 1:3).

I am not the Christ

WHY DID JOHN THE Baptist say "I am not the Christ"? Because he was not. And when we, as John the Baptists of this day, say "I am not the Christ," it can offend the listeners, because what power and reputation from Jesus' name that people can get, they take. John the Baptist did not, by the grace of God, try to get glory for himself.

But another question comes to mind in considering this text. Why did these people who came to John the Baptist even ask him if he was the Christ? (John 1:19–25). Was it because he seemed like it? If so, this ought to sober all of us. For if others confuse us with the Christ, for we are his brothers and sisters, having the same father and the same mother, we should ponder this. It is sobering. Because it means that if we are cruel to someone, they feel it as Christ being cruel to them. If we are unforgiving, they feel it as if Christ does not forgive them, as if he remembers them according to their sins. And if we greet them, when they are in darkness, Christ is calling them a brother or a sister when they are not. So then how would they ever know to repent?

If we do not retain, or hold as unpaid, the sin debt of another person that we know has not been cancelled, then how will they ever know their condition? Let us be pitiful and compassionate, and not lie to our fellow men. Let us say to them: "If ye were blind, ye should have no sin; but now ye say, 'We see'; therefore your sin remaineth" (John 9:41). For we ourselves have need of daily repentance, as Jesus tells us: "Or those eighteen, upon whom the tower in Siloam fell, and slew them, think ye that they were sinners above all men that dwelt in Jerusalem? I tell you, nay; but, except ye repent, ye shall all likewise perish" (Luke 13:4–5).

As for love, when we meet another person, let us think of them as someone that we owe a great debt to. Someone we need to repay. And that is the debt of love that we owe our neighbor. We always must feel as if we owe this debt to our fellow human beings. For they have all been redeemed, as we have been.

The fruits of repentance

Before David fell into adultery, the children of Israel were fighting the children of Ammon (2 Sam 10). We read that while David's soldiers went out to fight Ammon, "David tarried still at Jerusalem" (2 Sam 11:1).

So David should have gone to battle. But instead, he tarried at Jerusalem. Evil befell him. He fell into darkness. But after David received the grace of repentance, what were the fruits of that repentance? David

> gathered all the people together, and went to Rabbah, and fought against it, and took it. And he took their king's crown from off his head, the weight whereof was a talent of gold with the precious stones. And it was set on David's head. And he brought forth the spoil of the city in great abundance. And he brought forth the people that were therein, and put them under saws, and under harrows of iron, and under axes of iron, and made them pass through the brickkiln. And thus he did unto all the cities of the children of Ammon (2 Sam 12:29–31).

This is a beautiful picture of repentance. David went back to fix what had been left undone. He went back to battle. He put to death the things of the flesh. He was "always bearing about in the body the dying of the Lord Jesus, that the life also of Jesus might be made manifest in our body" (2 Cor 4:10). He put the crown of the foe on his head, to show that now by the Spirit he was ruling over his corrupt flesh, it did not rule him, for "if ye live after the flesh, ye shall die, but if ye through the Spirit do mortify the deeds of the body, ye shall live" (Rom 8:13).

David went back to battle and was "casting down imaginations, and every high thing that exalteth itself against the knowledge of God, and bringing into captivity every thought to the obedience of Christ" (2 Cor 10:5). Every thought, as every child of Ammon, was put under harrows.

Before David fell from faith, he was like Paul, saying: "I see another law in my members, warring against the law of my mind, and bringing me into captivity to the law of sin which is in my members" (Rom 7:23). But David lost this battle, and this understanding. Only when he, by God's power, was lifted from the dunghill, did he understand this battle again. Christ lived in him, and reigned in him. And through David's mouth, by the Spirit, Christ called to others: "As soon as they shall hear of me, they shall obey me. The strangers shall submit themselves unto me" (Ps 18:44). Jesus "being made perfect, became the author of eternal salvation unto all them that obey him" (Heb 5:9).

After he received the grace of repentance, David took up the cross and followed Christ. Once again he became an adversary to his flesh, as it is written: "But I keep under my body, and bring it into subjection. Lest that by any means, when I have preached to others, I myself should be a castaway" (1 Cor 9:27). Because we are commanded: "Mortify therefore your members which are upon the earth; fornication, uncleanness, ungodly affection, evil lasciviousness, and covetousness, which is idolatry" (Col 3:5). As it is written: "Dearly beloved, I beseech you as strangers and pilgrims, abstain from fleshly lusts, which war against the soul" (1 Pet 2:11).

Paul writes of the importance of war and battle. For we are a battling flock, fighting especially against the corruption that is in us:

> Being then made free from sin, ye became the slaves of righteousness. I speak after the manner of men because of the infirmity of your flesh. For as ye have yielded your members slaves to uncleanness and to iniquity unto

iniquity, even so now yield your members slaves of righteousness unto holiness (Rom 6:18–19).

In other words, a changed heart brings forth fruits. This is what happened to David. And others can see these fruits. For example, when one who has committed sins and wicked crimes against children receives the grace of repentance, he goes to the confessor father or mother and there receives atonement for all his sins, his unbelief. It is all forgiven. Then he leaves that person's home and his very next stop is the police station. He turns himself in at the police station and says, "I have committed crimes." And by this act, everyone knows that his repentance was indeed true, because it shows in the fruit of love for the neighbor, love of justice, respect for law and authority, reverence for the safety of young people and children, remorse. All these are fruits of a purified heart.

Lest ye be judged

"JUDGE NOT, THAT YE be not judged" (Matt 7:1) What is the judgment we speak of here? We shouldn't just dismiss this text or pass over it lightly. Because Paul takes up this same theme in the second chapter of Romans. Let's look carefully there in that second chapter. Do you remember how it is in the first chapter of Romans? Towards the end there is a list of sins:

> Being filled with all unrighteousness, fornication, wickedness, covetousness, maliciousness; full of envy, murder, debate, deceit, malignity; whisperers, backbiters, haters of God, despiteful, proud, boasters, inventors of evil things, disobedient to parents, without understanding, covenantbreakers, without natural affection, implacable, unmerciful.

Then it says of those who commit these sins, that they know "the judgment of God, that they which commit such things are worthy of death, not only do the same, but have pleasure in them that do them" (Rom 1:29–32). Thus ends the first chapter of Romans.

After listing out this condition of man and the fruit of his doings in his fallen state, what would you expect Paul to write next? Would you expect him to heap condemnation on those proud ones, boasters, murderers, unmerciful ones? For he says they are so bad, they do those things, they know the judgment of God that those who live in those works are worthy of death, but they not only do them, but have pleasure in those who do them. But what does Paul say after this?

In fact, in the second chapter, he turns to all people, Christians, non-Christians, all races, all creeds, and says: "You have no excuse, you who judge and condemn." He says, he who judges and condemns is condemning himself, because he does the same things. In other words, we all, by nature, are filled with unrighteousness, are gossipers, are proud, boasters, murderers. Paul goes on in the third chapter to cite Scripture showing how we are all under sin, evil and wicked.

So if we go about with a judgment-wishing mind towards the other, we are simply condemning ourselves. But if we go about with a mercy-wishing mind, knowing we ourselves are under the same condemnation and judgment unless God has mercy on us, we do well. For it is written: "For the Lord thy God is a merciful God; he will not forsake thee, neither destroy thee, nor forget the covenant of thy fathers which he sware unto them" (Deut 4:31). And the Psalmist sings: "Be merciful unto me; heal my soul, for I have sinned against thee" (Ps 41:4).

The lost sheep of the house of Israel

IT IS NOT STRANGE for us to first pray for our close ones who grew up in their childhood faith and left it some time in adulthood. Indeed, Jesus commands us: "Go first unto the lost sheep of the house of Israel" (Matt 10:6, 15:24).

Rebecca lamented to Isaac: "I am weary of my life because of the daughters of Heth" (Gen 27:46). She was moved to grief over the fate of Esau, and the wives he had taken from the world. Surely she cared about all the other people in this world, but it is not strange that she should be most deeply anguished by the loss of her close ones.

The same situation was with Samuel. He mourned for one close to him that he had lost. God asked Samuel: "How long wilt thou mourn for Saul?" (1 Sam 16:1). And the woman who had so little oil worried about her own dear sons who had become enslaved to the enemy (2 Kgs 4:1–5).

When someone has grown up in childhood faith, he does not forget it. The peace of his childhood home is never far from his thoughts (Luke 15:17). And he is never far from the thoughts of his heavenly father (Hos 11:8).

But God is merciful to sinners. God has been good to us. We, like our lost children who have left our midst, have been evil. And thus the Bible testifies of us: "What could have been done more to my vineyard, that I have not done in it? Wherefore, when I looked that it should bring forth grapes, brought it forth wild grapes?" (Isa 5:3–4). But God is merciful to us. And we know that God's chastisement has its effect. As it is written: "When he slew them, then they sought him, and they returned, and inquired early after God" (Ps 78:34).

Moses and the rock

WHY DID MOSES HIT the rock with his rod two times to get water (Num 20:11)? He was only supposed to hit it one time. We usually think of the water as the water of life. And we think of the rock (because of 1 Cor 10:4) as Christ. Then there is the rod, which is the staff of faith, upon which men have leaned (Gen 32:10, 47:31, Heb 11:21), and which opened the way through the sea (Exod 14:16, Neh 9:11), that sea which is death that drowns into perdition (Rom 6:4, Col 2:12, 1 Pet 3:21). Thus, using these various portions as our guide, it is a plausible explanation that the reason Moses hit the rock two times was because he lacked complete faith in the grace of God. Because of his lack of trust, he didn't strike the rock once, as he was commanded, but twice. In other words, simple faith (the rod), in Christ (the rock), to bring forth the stream of grace (the water). Beyond simple faith is "something more is required." This "something more" is a temptation to all of us. We demand, for example, stronger faith from others, or from ourselves. Or we lean into the law—we turn faith into a law, with all its fear and pretending. But the fact that Moses struck the rock two times rather than only once seems to signify a failing of faith. Because even for a moment, Moses' faith failed him, and he was not able to enter into the promised land. For he who doubts "is like a wave of the sea driven with the wind and tossed" (Jas 1:6).

A lack of faith is also a lack of patience, and this, I think, is another plausible explanation for what Moses was thinking when he hit that rock twice instead of once. Love "is not easily provoked" (1 Cor 13:5) but is patient (Heb 6:15). It is written: "We then that are strong ought to bear the infirmities of the weak, and not to please ourselves. Let every one of us please his neighbor for his good to edification" (Rom 15:1-2). But we are not loving and patient. We want results immediately. We carry the sickle when we should just be sowing seed. We are impatient. Moses could have been impatient too. This explanation of Moses striking the rock twice because of impatience fits with Numbers 11:10-15, where Moses gets impatient. So, in other words, he had faith, but he wanted to see results of faith, both in himself and in others, more quickly. But "the husbandman waiteth long for the harvest," (Jas 5:7), and Luke 13:6-9 also reminds us to be patient with others, as does the story of Abraham (Heb 6:15).

Moses struck the rock twice. Why? How do we teach this text? Well, as I have tried to demonstrate above, Scripture interprets Scripture. I gave two possible explanations for why Moses struck the rock twice. Now, there could be a perfectly good other reason that someone could give for why Moses hit the rock two times instead of once. And the other reason might be right. But the person who puts forth such an explanation, such a teaching, has the burden, as I do, of proving that his way of teaching this text is supported by other passages. And the more the other supporting passages, the better and stronger is his offering of how to teach the text to others.

Let us try a second example so we have a contrast. What can we teach from this passage: "And the dogs came and licked his sores" (Luke 16:21)? One possible teaching could be that the dogs picture the Gentiles. So the little dogs, which are often pictures of Gentiles, licked Lazarus's sores. So Lazarus, like Elijah (1 Kgs 17:6-9), was helped by Gentiles. In other words, the Gentiles had the gospel. If they didn't have the gospel, they would not have been able to help.

As for dogs licking sores, this is a commonly understood image from nature, from the natural world,—the licking of dogs can have medicinal qualities. So for Lazarus, the Gentiles did the binding up of oozing sores that Isaiah talks about in his first chapter: "From the sole of the foot even unto the head there is no soundness in it, but wounds, and bruises, and putrefying sores. They have not been closed, neither bound up, neither mollified with ointment" (Isa 1:6).

The question at hand is, what other texts support the understanding that this text is to teach us that Lazarus was helped by Gentiles, that is, Lazarus was helped by people who are often looked down on, people who are thought of as being "unworthy of the kingdom of God"? If my explanation of this text is a good one, then this text is a good warning, and a teaching that fits with Romans 11. Because there, Paul strongly exhorts those who have the gospel not to look down on those who don't. But, as we see, this is what happens all the time. We, who have the gospel, think we will always have it, because we are so good and better than those Gentile dogs, and "sinners" as Paul reminds us (Gal 2:15), sarcastically throwing our self-righteous designations back at us. It's true that Paul was a Jew, but the lesson is not so much about Jews and Gentiles as it is about those who are of Israel in heart and those who are not. Texts warning the "Jews" not to be proud in their chosen-ness mean nothing to Jews today, because those who are Jews by nature are lost right now. But whoever is one of the elect today, who does not take these warnings about pride and smugness to heart, these texts are for him. He is in a dangerous place. For the text about the dogs licking Lazarus's sores should sober us all, reminding us that those we think are dogs, who are gross sinners, will enter into the kingdom of God before us, if we are scribes and Pharisees (Matt 21:31). We must have the perfect righteousness of Christ to enter into the kingdom: "For I say unto you, that except your righteousness shall exceed the righteousness of the scribes and Pharisees, ye shall in no case enter into the kingdom of heaven" (Matt 5:20).

I think my first example above is more solid. In other words, my explanations for why Moses struck the rock two times is supported by many other passages. I think the second example is a little bit more of a reach, but I offer it to you so you can read the Scriptures yourself, interpreting each text in the context of the entire contents of Scripture, and not put forth an explanation of a text that is not easily connected to and understood by other passages.

The work of theology

THE WORK OF THEOLOGY, or the work of public space speaking of matters of the heart, is also the work of choosing certain words or images or word-assemblies and avoiding others. There are many word-assemblies in Scripture. The writer of the letter to the Hebrews says that Genesis 22, the story of Abraham offering up Isaac, is a parable. That is what the Greek word in Hebrews 11:19 translated in the KJV as "figure," means. Thus, we have an entire story, or anecdote about an event in a person's life, which we are to think of as a parable. It is a lesson, it is something taken from natural life, from visible things. It is to point us to the matters of the heart, to the matters of eternity, to the place beyond the border of time, to the things that are invisible. The entire tabernacle and worship service described in Exodus and Leviticus are also called a parable in Greek, which is in the KJV also translated "figure" (Heb 9:9).

Other sections of texts, or word-assemblies, besides those that appear to us as "stories," exist in the Bible. Laws, for example. Luther says in his commentary on Deuteronomy, for example, that the law about freeing a Hebrew slave (Deut 15:12–18, Exod 21:1–6) is to teach us, among other things, about the invisible, that is, the truth that a man who has been brought out of slavery to sin nevertheless becomes a slave to others in love. That person willingly, and happily, and voluntarily, enslaves, or subdues, his flesh, as Paul writes in 1 Corinthians 9:27: "But I keep under my body, and bring it into subjection: lest that by any means, when I have preached to others, I myself should be a castaway."

So the whole Bible is words or word-assemblies (allegories) that make up parables, or stories, that are to point us to Christ and the truth of his kingdom, his reign.

A theologian should choose word-assemblies and parables that the Scripture chooses, for the most part. And if he makes up something different, he should be able to point to Scriptural foundations for what he makes up new. Also, the images, or word-assemblies from the natural world that Scripture chooses often, the theologian should learn and investigate these well. Take, for example, the Song of Solomon. The Scripture devotes an entire book to one item from the natural world, love, or married love. One could almost think that the Holy Spirit was thinking, "Why should the devil get all the good metaphors?" So God took this central item from human existence and spent a lot of time using it to teach.

What about slavery? Is this not something commonly known among all peoples and cultures? Moses teaches with this concept, counseling us to remember how the jubilee, which is the year of release from debt-slavery, is the era of grace, because in the house of the Son of God we have always the ongoing and continual forgiveness of sins. Debts that are incurred daily are daily forgiven, so that our pending sale to the enemy for payment of our debts never happens. And to be slaves in Egypt is what we truly deserve. But Moses goes on to teach how the debts of strangers are not forgiven. This is to remind all people that there is no forgiveness of sins on the outside of the kingdom of God. For the Son of God testifies that "he that abideth in me, and I in him, the same bringeth forth much fruit: for without me ye can do nothing" (John 15:5). And we know from Scripture that "the Lord said unto Moses, 'Whosoever hath sinned against me, him will I blot out of my book'" (Exod 32:33). And we know that "whosoever was not found written in the book of life was cast into the lake of fire" (Rev 20:15).

Thus we constantly go about reminding those who are not of faith, who are bound in their sins, in debt-slavery, that they do owe, and they must pay to the last farthing. "Verily I say unto thee, thou shalt by no means come out thence, till thou hast paid the uttermost farthing" (Matt 5:26). Thus they will realize their condition and repent.

There are many figures and parables, or word-assemblies, that the Bible uses to teach us. The above are only a few. And we know, as Proverbs 1:5–6 says: "A wise man will hear, and will increase learning; and a man of understanding shall attain unto wise counsels: to understand a proverb, and the interpretation, the words of the wise, and their dark sayings."

Why do bad things happen?

A TEACHING IN ACTS 28 is that Fate, or Justice on this earth, does not "catch up" with people who sin, and that sin catching up with them is not why bad things happen to people. But Genesis 19 shows that bad things happen to people because of the sins of the people. How do we reconcile these two texts? For we know that the people of Sodom were wicked sinners, and their cry (Gen 18:20–21) went up to God. And eventually, the measure of sin was filled up so full for these people that God annihilated them because of their sins. Notice that this seems to contradict Acts 28. There, the barbarians think that a snake bites a person to punish him for his evil deeds. And if the bite does not kill the person, it is because the person wasn't such an evil person after all.

Again, the teachings seem to contradict. For in the one, sin is pointed to as the cause, and punishment is meted out. And in the other, Paul says, no, you can't point to the evil in man as the cause for why a specific event happened to him. But the key here is cause and effect. We cannot point to specific events with perfect knowledge of cause and effect unless, as with Genesis 19, we are told to. In general, sins catch up with people and cause misery (Num 32:23). But in general, the wicked also flourish (Ps 73:5, 12, Jer 12:2) in this life, and have very little misery that we can see.

We ought not point to specific cases of misery, we should only make general statements, unless, as I said above, we know from God's Word that we can make statements about specific cases. For example, if someone said today that Sodom and Gomorrah were destroyed because of the sins of the people, we should agree with them. But if some bomb were dropped somewhere or something horrific happened to some group of people, we should not therefore think that it is because these people deserved it more, that they were worse sinners than we are. We can only state that in general, bad things happen, evil is in this world and causes us misery because we are all so sinful and miserable (Rom 3:10–18).

The sin of wanting

ONCE I SAW A person say about the Muslim idea of heaven that it was something to be desired greatly. This man was not a Muslim but his words revealed a great deal to me. How is the Muslim conception of heaven pleasing? It is carnal, neighbor-hating, and it tramples all over marriage. So how can someone want that? How can it be thought of with longing? Wouldn't one's love for marriage, and one's love for the Word of God, make someone hate the Muslim conception of heaven?

But isn't everything about wanting? It's not what we *do*, it's what we *want* to do. And you can tell what is in people's hearts not only by what they do and say, but by what they get angry about. In other words, often I see that a person is not sad, or grieved, over sin that another person does. Instead he is angry. He is almost jealous. He is often angry simply because he wishes he could do those sins, and get away with them. But what of the person whose reaction is not anger? What if his reaction is sadness? He grieves that sin got committed, that someone got hurt. And he does not want to do the sin himself, and never did want to. He is not angry. He is sad. He sighs and cries (Ezek 9:4). This is why, as has been often noticed, people's reactions to the Scripture are so revealing. And even in Scripture, people's reactions to events are revealing as well. For example, Simon and Levi's reaction to what happened to their sister in Genesis 34. They were very angry. By this anger they showed how evil had overtaken their heart. Because they said: "Should he treat her as one treats a whore?" Therefore "cursed is their anger" (Gen 49:7). They were just upset that they couldn't sin like the "heathen" and get away with it. In any case, they were angry. Either out of jealousy or desire for revenge, perhaps. But Jacob was just sad. That was all. Why? Because Jacob never wanted to have women wrongly. He was never in that horrid competition.

It is all about wanting. Again, it's not what we *do* that's important, it is what we *want* to do. We are all actors, hypocrites. But how will that help us on the last day? How will it help us to say, "I did such and such good things all my life?" God knows perfectly well that we wanted to do and live entirely differently. But we feared.

The only way to not want what you ought not want is to get a new heart (Ezek 36:26). That is, to turn, to repent, to change your whole self. And only God can do this. And even if we do, by the grace of God, get a new heart, what do we find? Do we find that we are like Lot and cannot even imagine to do evil? Or do we say with Paul that what I do not want to do, that I do. There is still a law in us that hates God, and hates all that is good and holy. And it clings to us unto the grave. May God help us! "For thine arrows stick fast in me, and thy hand presseth me sore" (Ps 38:2). And God will help us: "As for thee, by the blood of thy covenant I have sent forth thy prisoners out of the pit wherein is no water. Turn you to the strong hold, ye prisoners of hope, even today do I declare that I will render double unto thee" (Zech 9:11–12).

Openly and publicly

JESUS IS THE SHEPHERD of the congregation, and its king (Num 27:16–17). He is the head of the body; the church is his body (Eph 1:22–23, 4:15–16, Col 1:18). The congregation judges according to the Word; it is the pillar and ground of truth. The congregation is called "the house of God" and "the church of the living God" (1 Tim 3:15). It is written about the importance of the judgment of the congregation: "And they shall be unto you cities for refuge from the avenger; that the manslayer die not, until he stand before the congregation in judgment" (Num 35:12). And: "Then the congregation shall judge between the slayer and the revenger of blood according to these judgments" (Num 35:24). Notice it says "according to these judgments." For there is no difference between the judgment of the congregation and the judgment of Scripture.

The congregation is separate and holy, as it is written: "For how shall it be known here that I and your people have found grace in your sight? Is it not in that you go with us? So shall we be separated, I and your people, from all the people that are upon the face of the earth" (Exod 33:16, cf. Num 23:9, Exod 19:5, 1 Pet 2:9). All who are in the congregation are abiding in the forgiveness of sins (Lev 16:24, Num 15:26, 16:47, Heb 13:12). And so they are all holy. When Korah said that the entire congregation is holy (Num 16:3), he spoke rightly. It was just that he was not himself part of the congregation of God; he was in the congregation of wickedness, as events showed. For the congregation consists of all the people who have the Holy Spirit in their hearts, and therefore they are all enlightened (Exod 10:23). They all have a holy fear of God (Exod

34:30). They obey and do his Word (Exod 39:42; 1 John 5:2). It is true that each member is sinful and deserving only of the wrath of God, but sin is not imputed unto them when, through the power of the Spirit of grace, they have faith in Christ's redemption work. Therefore the congregation of God is still holy, even in the midst of the uncleanness of the people (Lev 16:16); for "through [Christ] we both have access by one Spirit unto the Father" (Eph 2:18).

Therefore we ought to trust the voice of the congregation, which is the Spirit and the Word. We ought to let this living Word in the congregation speak on matters, for all are equal, and matters concern everybody, and all people on earth ought to hear, and learn, in the congregation. Jeremiah spoke in the temple to all who came (Jer 26:2). Ezra brought the teaching of God before the congregation, before all, for all who could hear (Neh 8:2). Joel preached that the congregation should be gathered and sanctified and assembled; they all needed to hear (Joel 2:16). Aaron, who blessed all the people (Lev 9:22), spoke to all the people about the things God had told Moses concerning their deliverance from Egypt (Exod 4:30–31).

In the story of the sin of Achan, the matter was brought to light in the presence of all the people, not just some of them (Josh 7:13–18). When there was a difference between Saul and Jonathan on the matter of where and how we receive strength, the matter was made clear in the presence of all the people (1 Sam 14:42–45). News of how the Word of God had gone forth was told before all the church by Paul and those who were with him (Acts 14:27).

God speaks at the door of the Tent of Meeting, which is also translated "Tabernacle of the Congregation" (Exod 29:42), and God says that he speaks in the congregation, especially at the mercy seat (Exod 25:22, Num 7:89). God's glory dwells in, and speaks in, the congregation (Exod 40:35, Num 20:6–7). We ought to listen to the voice of God as it comes through the Spirit in the gathered assembly. For the Spirit teaches the Word. The Spirit in the congregation is in perfect agreement with the Word at all times (Isa 8:16).

It is important that we always be free, and open, and public. When the children of Israel murmured against Moses and Aaron in the wilderness, Moses addressed the matter openly and publicly. He told Aaron: "Say to the whole congregation of the people of Israel, 'Come near before the Lord, for he has heard your murmuring'" (Exod 16:2, 9). Moses also spoke to the entire congregation about the rules for the Passover in Exodus 12:3.

Many times Moses gathered together the entire congregation and spoke to them (Exod 14:13, 16:6, 35:1, 4, Lev 8:3–5, 9:5, 23, 11:2, 17:2, 24, 19:2, Num 11:18, 24, 14:39, Deut 2:4, 4:10, 31:30). Sometimes he called just the elders (Exod 34:31, Num 11:16, cf. Num 32:2), but for the most part he spoke much to the entire congregation. And when Moses called the elders, he called all of them, not just some of them. Others besides Moses brought matters forward, but it was to the entire congregation (Num 14:7, 15:33, Deut 27:1, Josh 1:10–11, 8:35). This is because every person needs to hear, and fear, and learn, not just a few of them, as it is written: "And all the people shall hear, and fear, and do no more presumptuously" (Deut 17:13). Since every temptation is common to every man (1 Cor 10:13), all can benefit from hearing instruction, all are equal. God commands that what is spoken be spoken to everybody (Deut 1:3, 20:2, Isa 57:19, Luke 2:10, 24:47, Acts 10:36, 2 Cor 5:19–20). It is written in one of the songs at the end of Deuteronomy: "Yea, he loved the people; all his saints are in thy hand; and they sat down at thy feet; every one shall receive of thy words" (33:3). And in Acts: "For the promise is unto you, and to your children, and to all that are afar off, even as many as the Lord our God shall call" (2:39).

Deuteronomy 31:12 says: "Gather the people together, men, and women, and children, and thy stranger that is within thy gates." Why? So they can hear, so they can learn, so they fear the Lord, and observe to do all the words of his teaching.

Comments on Genesis translations

THE NEW INTERNATIONAL VERSION (NIV) translation of the Bible translates Genesis 3:1 using the word "crafty" instead of "subtle," which is the word the King James Version (KJV) uses. This is a typical example of where the NIV is better than the KJV. Meanings of words can change over time, and the word "subtle" does not mean what it meant in 1611 when the KJV was published. The NIV was published a few decades ago.

But let us continue on in Genesis, comparing the NIV to the KJV. The NIV in Genesis 3:6 has "the fruit of the tree was good for food and pleasing to the eye." The KJV margin note there says that the tree was "a desire to the eye," which is more literal to the Hebrew. If one prefers literalness wherever one can have it and still make sense, one will tend to prefer the KJV.

And in 3:7 the NIV has "the eyes of both of them were opened, and they realized they were naked." The KJV has "knew" instead of "realized," which is better on the whole. But I can understand a choice of "realized." Use of the word "knew" is slightly more literal though, and the writer of Genesis is playing on this word "know" and "knowledge," so it is too bad not to reflect that in the English, when it can easily be done.

In Genesis 3:8 the NIV says, "then the man and his wife heard the sound of the Lord God as he was walking in the garden." Here, since the "voice of the Lord" is what the Hebrew says, and because the "voice of the Lord" is so important in the rest of Scripture, it is too bad the NIV translators didn't do as the KJV translators did, and have something like: "And they heard the voice of the Lord

God walking...". This reflects beautifully Isaiah 52:7: "How beautiful upon the mountains are the feet of him that bringeth good tidings." For Genesis 3:8 says that there is a voice walking. We must all hear and heed God's voice, and it comes to us on the feet of men (Rom 10:14-15). Also: "Now then we are ambassadors for Christ, as though God did beseech you by us" (2 Cor 5:20). It is not the many *sounds* God makes or doesn't make that we care about. It is his *voice* that we are to concern ourselves with: "Ye heard the voice of the words, but saw no similitude; only ye heard a voice." (Deut 4:12). It was the voice of God at Mount Sinai, "a great voice" (Deut 5:22). It was the "still small voice" that Elijah heard (1 Kgs 19:12). It was heard at Jesus' baptism and his transfiguration. It is still heard today.

In Genesis 4:1 the NIV translates: "Adam made love to his wife Eve." Since the original Hebrew says "knew" as the KJV has it, "Adam knew Eve his wife," why change it? That old way was perfect. I suppose the translators thought it would help the reader understand better, but it is too bad they didn't trust the reader more. I also like the KJV in this verse because it has "his wife" at the end, as a sort of emphasis. That is, God commands us to know only our wife, not some other woman.

In Genesis 4:4 the NIV is very good, translating: "The Lord looked with favor on Abel and his offering." The reader will much better understand what is meant than by the KJV: "And the Lord had respect unto Abel and to his offering." However, I wish the NIV would have said, "looked with grace." And, the KJV has the benefit of echoing perfectly Numbers 16:15, where Moses refers to this verse from Genesis, quoting it directly. It's too bad the NIV translators of Genesis didn't try harder to better reflect Numbers 16:15. In the end though, you can't use the word "respect" anymore, in the sense it is used here, because it doesn't mean what it meant in 1611. For example, Exodus 2:25 is simply awful in the KJV: "And God looked upon the children of Israel, and God had respect unto them." It should be something like this: "And God looked upon the children of Israel, and God knew."

In Genesis 4:7 I don't know what to think. The NIV does very well in translating: "You must rule over [sin]." This is good. This is a command. Cain found he could not follow the command of God, but God does command us to rule over sin. When we hear this command we ought to despair of ourselves and run to the mercy seat. But as Cain, we do not. So to have this plainly stated, "You must rule over [sin]" is most excellent.

In Genesis 4:8 the NIV interprets, "rose up against" as "attacked," but it seems as if it would have been better if they had followed closer to the original more literally as the KJV does, since we all know what "rose up against" means, and this way of speaking is common in the Bible. To rise up implies that you were low. Thus, to rise up against means going from being among the meek to rising to go against God. For the people rose up against God, though they said they rose up against Moses (Num 16:11).

It is too bad in Genesis 6:3 the NIV doesn't translate "flesh" as "flesh." Instead they say "mortal." "Flesh" is a very good translation, and very literal, and it answers to other usages: "that which is flesh is flesh" (John 3:6) and "flesh and blood cannot inherit the kingdom of God" (1 Cor 15:50) and "I know that in me (that is, in my flesh,) dwelleth no good thing" (Rom 7:18) and many other similar places. In the sacrificial worship service, there is a slaying of the flesh, a burning of it, which is a picture of Christ's work, which he did, in the flesh (Rom 8:3), slaying, crucifying, the flesh, the old Adam in us, which is not just *mortal*, it is *carnal*. The whole point of having sacrificial worship service from Adam's first altar until the destruction of the second temple was to teach this truth, so it is unfortunate if a translation sidles around it. The KJV is relatively consistent in translating the Hebrew word "flesh" and the Greek word "flesh," and it works very well. "Forasmuch then as Christ hath suffered for us in the flesh, arm yourselves likewise with the same mind; for he that hath suffered in the flesh hath ceased from sin" (1 Pet 4:1). Also: "Knowing this, that our old man is crucified with him, that the body of sin might be destroyed" (Rom 6:6).

The NIV says in Genesis 6:4 "the Nephilim" were on the earth in those days. Why not translate the Hebrew word? Or at least put it as a mandatory footnote? Say that "the Fallen Ones were on the earth in those days." Also in this verse, I could never figure out why the KJV translates the end of this verse "men of reknown" when it seems more straightforward to translate as "men of the name." But the KJV is nice compared to the NIV here because both here in Genesis 6:4 and Numbers 16:2 they translate "men of the name" as "men of reknown." Thus these two passages allude to each other, as they should. The NIV loses all this complementary sound by translating Numbers 16:2, "well-known community leaders who had been appointed members of the council."

Genesis 6:6 is hard. The NIV translates: "The Lord regretted that he had man human beings on the earth." The KJV says: "And it repented the Lord that he had made man on the earth." Maybe it could be something like "the Lord was sorry" that he had made man on the earth.

In Genesis 6:8 obviously the KJV is better, more theological, in translating that "Noah found grace in the eyes of the Lord." The NIV says: "But Noah found favor in the eyes of the Lord."

In Genesis 8:21 neither the NIV or the KJV is close enough to the original Hebrew for me. The KJV says that "the Lord smelled a sweet savor," and the NIV says: "the Lord smelled the pleasing aroma." The best way to get at the Hebrew might be: "The Lord smelled a sweet smell of rest." Thus the reader would understand that it is the smell of the eternal rest in Christ that is in question. The KJV translation hints at this understanding, because both here and in 2 Corinthians 2:15 they translate "sweet savor," so that the one passage reflects the other, as they are meant to. This is well done. The KJV translates 2 Corinthians 2:15: "For we are unto God a sweet savor of Christ, in them that are saved, in them that perish."

In Genesis 9:23 the NIV says: "But Shem and Japheth took a garment and laid it across their shoulders; then they walked backward and covered their father's naked body. Their faces were turned the other way so that they would not see their father naked." Why did they add in the word "body"? It is not in the Hebrew. It is nakedness that is spoken of here. And to translate it to reflect strongly the idea of nakedness answers well to the rest of Scripture, for example in Revelations: "That the shame of thy nakedness do not appear" (3:18).

Neither the NIV or the KJV satisfies in the translation of Genesis 9:27, though the KJV margin note does well. God is promising to one day persuade Japheth, to call some from Japheth unto himself. God calls by gentle persuasion and love, even as Hosea 2 shows, among many other places. In any case, the KJV translates Genesis 9:27 as "God shall enlarge Japheth" and the NIV says: "May God extend Japheth's territory." The Hebrew verb means "persuade," but translators have often thought there must be an error in the marking of the Hebrew vowel, so they have changed it to "expand" or "enlarge." It's too bad.

In Genesis 11:1 the NIV translates: "Now the whole world had one language and a common speech." I wish they would not put "common" in there. It seems to me that this implies that "common" is in the original. Why not translate more simply as the KJV does: "And the whole world was of one language, and of one speech"? I suppose choices had to be made and I'm sure the translators were doing their best as they knew how to do it. Notice, though, how good verse 6 sounds in the KJV, repeating the "one." It says: "And the Lord said, 'Behold, the people is one, and they have all one language . . . '". Notice also how at the end of this verse the KJV has "which they have imagined to do." The Hebrew has a negative connotation, as the KJV does, also the KJV, by translating "imagined," hearkens the reader back to Genesis 6:5 and 8:21 where it speaks of how the imagination, or thoughts and intents of the heart of man, are evil from his youth. This shadowing and layering and word-reminding is so often lost in the NIV.

Clearly the NIV is better in Genesis 11:7 because the modern reader of English needs to know that "confuse" is what is meant by the Hebrew. Nowadays "confound" is not used so much in the sense of "confuse."

In Genesis 12:15 the NIV is very clear and well done: "And when Pharaoh's officials saw her, they praised her to Pharaoh." However, in Genesis 12:1, why don't they keep "plagued," which can mean something medical, but can also mean something of the soul? Instead they translate in the NIV: "But the Lord inflicted serious diseases on Pharaoh," which, besides being ugly, doesn't hearken the reader's mind to the story of the Exodus, as this story is meant to do. Besides, it almost limits everything to a medical explanation, which is not necessary.

The Hebrew of Genesis 13:8 says "for we are men, brethren." The NIV obscures this by translating "for we are close relatives." This is a mistake. For we who are as Abraham and Lot, we are brothers and sisters and joint-heirs of eternal life. This is shown beautifully in Genesis 31. There, Laban and Laban's brothers are following Jacob. The word "brother" is used in verses 23, 25, 32, 37, and 46. Finally, in verse 54 we read: "Then Jacob offered sacrifice upon the mount, and called his brethren to eat bread." Now who would Jacob's brothers be? Not Esau, surely—he was not there. But all who were of Laban's crowd who humbled themselves and repented, slaughtering their old man and wishing to rise up in the new man through the sacrificial work of God, those were Jacob's brothers. And they ate with him. Laban did not. This is an example of how nice it is when translators are more literal, which the NIV does not do, translating those places "relatives."

I wish the KJV and the NIV would have translated Genesis 14:24 "young boy," and "grape-cluster," instead of "Aner" and "Eshcol."

The NIV is very nice and a great improvement over the KJV in Genesis 15:2, where they translate what the KJV translates "steward" as "the one who will inherit my estate."

But the NIV is flat wrong in Genesis 16:6. Sarah did not mistreat Hagar. She afflicted her. Affliction can be good or bad. Paul writes of "our light affliction," for example (2 Cor 4:17). God afflicts in love, but he does not mistreat us (Rev 3:19). Sarah chastised and afflicted in love so that Hagar would come to the knowledge of her condition. This is a picture of what God does for us many times: "My son, despise not the chastening of the Lord; neither be weary of his correction" (Prov 3:11). Sarah did not mistreat any more than Joseph did when he played a seemingly harsh game with his brothers. He wanted them to call to mind their sin, which they did remember, as we see in Genesis 42:21–22. This is what kind of heart Sarah had for Hagar. But Hagar fled. Notice the angel of the Lord advised her to go back to Sarah and submit to her. And notice that Hagar never did.

See how beautiful the KJV is in Genesis 18:5: "and comfort ye your hearts." Also in Genesis 19:19: "And thou hast magnified they mercy, which thou hast shewed unto me in saving my life." The NIV says: "You have shown great kindness to me." But everyone knows the KJV always wins when it comes to the question of beauty of language.

The NIV is very nice in Genesis 20:5: "I have done this with a clean conscience and clean hands." But in Genesis 20:13 it should be: "And this is the grace that you will show to me," but the KJV has "kindness" and the NIV has "love." But perhaps this goes back to Luther's influence, because he was sometimes a lousy translator of the word "grace" from Hebrew.

What are we to conclude? We can conclude with Luther that one word badly translated can cause confusion in all of Scripture. We can also conclude with Luther that nobody can be much of a theologian if he does not learn Greek and/or Hebrew. That is our best hope with meeting with situations of debate such as described between the KJV and the NIV.

The secrets of men

ONE OF THE MOST common ways people misread the Bible is by identifying themselves with the wrong person. They do not think they are the friend in Matthew 22:12, they think they are one of the safe ones. They read about the Last Supper and they picture themselves as being one of the eleven disciples. They do not imagine themselves there at the Last Supper as being Judas. And even in this story of the Last Supper they do not comprehend that if they are truly identifying themselves as being one of the disciples, then they have to assume that they are likely to be Judas. For to be in heart and mind a disciple, one of the eleven, you have to have the heart and mind of one who believes that he is very likely to be Judas. For if you do not read with a dull mind, you perceive that the disciples *all* asked Jesus, "Lord, is it I?" (Matt 26:22). They were very sure that it was very likely that they were the betrayer, not the others. Not that one, but me. I did it.

A child of God, a disciple of Jesus, believes he is saved. He also believes that he is close to becoming a Judas, and begs God for mercy daily to keep him from that path. Probably the most memorable example of this heart of a disciple is the example of King David. As he was chased in the wilderness he continuously held that he, David, could easily fall to be as Saul. As he testified: "There is but a step between me and death" (1 Sam 20:3). It was the case with David as it was with Paul. As it is written: "But we had the sentence of death in ourselves, that we should not trust in ourselves, but in God which raiseth the dead; who delivered us from so great a death, and doth deliver: in whom we trust that he will yet deliver us" (2 Cor 1:9–10).

David would not lift his hand against Saul (1 Sam 24:6,10). And he said: "Destroy him not, for who can stretch forth his hand against the Lord's anointed, and be guiltless?" (1 Sam 26:9). How sad that we do not do as David did! David did not wish to rashly judge and condemn Saul. He waited for God's time. But we are very swift to judge and condemn other people. That is, we are swift to judge and condemn, unless we think that we ourselves are likely to fall and be in the position of Saul. David hoped even when he had no evidence to point to hope. He hoped that Saul could rise up from the grave and live again in grace. When the doctrine of the Amalek came, David opposed it. For the doctrine of the Amalek is that there is no hope. It is the doctrine of Cain which says that the sin is too great to be forgiven (Gen 4:13). The Amalek said of Saul: "I was sure that he could not live after that he was fallen" (2 Sam 1:10). By this testimony the Amalek shows that he was abiding in death and the doctrines of death, which are unto condemnation. This man of Amalek died without mercy, for he was unmerciful (2 Sam 1:16, cf. Matt 18:33–34). It is written: "Blessed *is* he that considereth the poor; the Lord will deliver him in time of trouble" (Ps 41:1). The doctrine of Amalek does not consider the poor, does not consider itself to be a Judas, or a Saul, and so the people who follow this teaching of Amalek condemn their own souls by their sentences of judgment and death on this earth to others. The doctrine of Amalek holds no hope for those who have fallen away, that they can return, as the prodigal son. But to the upright "there ariseth light in the darkness; *he is* gracious, and full of compassion, and righteous" (Ps 112:4).

Let's take another example, that of the puffed-up, proud super-apostles of Corinth. When we read about them, we immediately identify ourselves with Apostle Paul, instead of the super-apostles. When warned of being puffed-up, we don't take to heart the truth that it is *us* who are puffed-up. Instead we read the books of Corinthians and piously look around us and notice how puffed-up and proud some of our neighbors are. And sometimes we get so bad we go around telling others about them. And we accuse them of pride, if not out loud, then in our minds: "That person has grown in himself. He is proud." We read about the people who said: "We will not hearken" (Jer 6:17), and we consider ourselves to be in the place of Jeremiah, not in the place of the people—we don't think, when we read "we will not hearken," that the text is speaking about *us*. We think it is speaking about other people, and we are upset with them. This is a grave error that we make. Notice that Nehemiah did not make this error (Neh 9:36–37).

When we know that it says at the end of 1 Corinthians 4 to "put away from among yourselves that wicked person," we quickly agree to ostracizing another person, or telling others to keep them under suspicion—but what if it was us? What if we read 1 Corinthians 4 and decided that Paul was talking about me—that the gathering of God's children should put me away and out from among them? For a little leaven leavens the whole lump.

You can see how proud and self-assured we all are, for if you are like me, in reading 1 Corinthians 4 it never crossed your mind to be anywhere but in the throng of people who are casting the other one out.

What is to be done with us? What is to be done with our hard-hearted hatred towards our neighbor? Our smug accusing minds? It feels futile, and I fear that we shall all go to our graves with "divisions" amongst ourselves, not understanding ourselves to be all equally guilty, and that our only redemption and wisdom and sanctification is an alien righteousness, which is not ours—we wear it as we wear a robe. It covers our nakedness, but the nakedness is still there—it is just not made manifest.

I can illustrate how impossible we all are by a story. Vaino Havas wrote many stories. One popular one while I was growing up was a story written to illustrate the parable of the sower. At the end of the story Havas has the main character, a pastor, sit down with just one of the four young people who each illustrate one of the four kinds of soil (heart-soil). The pastor tells the boy: "Only for you do I have hope." Now we all have read this story many times, and nobody has noticed how evil a thing this is for the pastor to be saying this to the boy. The pastor had decided this boy was "good soil" and that the other three were not. Just imagine if the pastor had said: "Go steal and lie and commit adultery." We would all have immediately recognized what he said as evil. But for years, we just pass by this pastor who, god-like, had taken it upon himself to decide the conditions of people's hearts. And worse, he had given up hope on three souls that Christ purchased with his own blood.

Notice that the stories of the sower that Jesus told as they appear in the Bible do not at all invite us to decide what kind of heart is before us. And yet we do it all the time. We are just like that pastor in Havas's story. We are all Jonahs, hating other people—only happy that the people we like, that we prefer, receive the grace of repentance, and having no hope for those who we decide are bad soil and beyond hope.

Notice how much this goes against love and grace. It is a sin not to have hope for the soul of another. It's also smug and proud, because in effect we are saying: "God can easily save me, but that other guy—no, he's gone too far." Thus we all have the mind of Cain, claiming that "the sin is too great to be forgiven" (Gen 4:13).

When will we become disciples? When will we understand and have compassion? It is God who judges between the cattle and the cattle, between the rams and the great he-goats (Ezek 34:17). Not us. "For thou, even thou only, knowest the hearts of all the children of men" (1 Kgs 8:39). And: "I know the things that come into your mind, every one of them" (Ezek 11:5).

If we judge, then let us judge ourselves to be the greatest he-goat, the Balaam, the Korah, the Saul. Let us fear "the day when God shall judge the secrets of men" (Rom 2:16). And let us confess that we boast in God and say that we know his will and are confident that we are a guide to the blind, but we break the law, and dishonor God. What fools. What hypocrites. A generation of vipers. "Since the days of our fathers we have been in a great trespass unto this day; and for our iniquities have we, our kings, and our priests, been delivered into the hand of the kings of the lands, to the sword, to captivity, and to a spoil, and to confusion of face, as it is this day" (Ezra 9:7).

Visitation for a nation or people

THERE COMES A TIME that God calls out to a nation. He hopes that they will blush over their sins and repent and be saved. But sometimes the people do not listen. Then, it can happen that the day of visitation is over in that area. As it is written: "Were they ashamed when they had committed abomination? Nay, they were not at all ashamed, neither could they blush. Therefore they shall fall among them that fall. In the time of their visitation they shall be cast down" (Jer 8:12). When God draws his kingdom away from an area, there is no more pardoning. Then for that people it is as it is written: "We have transgressed and have rebelled. Thou hast not pardoned" (Lam 3:42).

How sad to be in such a state that God has forsaken so terribly! It is written about such people that "they shall go with their flocks, and with their herds, to seek the Lord. But they shall not find him. He hath withdrawn himself from them" (Hos 5:6).

God's wrath comes unto them to the uttermost. As it is written: "And I will dash them one against another, even the fathers and the sons together, saith the Lord. I will not pity, nor spare, nor have mercy, but destroy them" (Jer 13:14).

In the Bible, the 109th psalm is applied to Satan's own in Acts 1:16–26. How sad for those forsaken by the Lord, whose sins still stand condemning them! Of them it is said: "Let the iniquity of his fathers be remembered with the Lord, and let not the sin of his mother be blotted out" (Ps 109:14).

This exact fate will happen to us if we do not repent and run to the wounds of Jesus. For our doings are all entirely always evil.

May we heed these words of Scripture: "Execute judgment in the morning, and deliver him that is spoiled out of the hand of the oppressor, lest my fury go out like fire, and burn that none can quench it, because of the evil of your doings" (Jer 21:12).

Women as priests

As I have always taught and said, openly and publicly, nowhere in the Scriptures do we see women as priests. We see women as prophets, teachers, judges, and administrators. But never as priests.

It seems to me that in an extreme situation, where a priest called by the congregation is not available, and there is some emergency, like a necessary baptism, an older woman could function as a priest and read the baptismal rituals. But even this is a stretch because all little babies, baptized or not, are saved. So the only reason I could see an old woman having to act as priest for a few moments is because of the weak faith of the parents, who simply need the ritual of the baptism. But even in that case, a simple lesson from the Word of God assuring the listeners that the unbaptized dead child is in the bosom of Abraham would be better.

Huldah was a prophetess (2 Kgs 22:14, 2 Chr 34:22). Philip's daughters prophesied (Acts 21:9). Priscilla seems to have functioned as the administrator of the congregation (Rom 16:3, Phil 4:3), a sort of chairman of the board. Paul writes that "a woman should keep silence in church" (1 Cor 14:34), which seems to imply that no woman should be doing anything that causes offense or disturbances, because Paul can't mean that a woman can never speak in church, because he says that they do pray and prophesy (1 Cor 11:5). In any case, Paul had no problem with Priscilla (Acts 18:26) or Philip's daughters, that we know of. And he advised Timothy that older women should teach some of the people (Titus 2:4). Many unnamed women seemed to have prophesied, according to the Bible (Joel 2:28, Acts 2:17). Isaiah's wife is called a prophetess (Isa 8:3).

When considering this issue, as with any other issue, we can't just take one passage from the Scripture and say, "this is what the Scripture teaches." For the Scripture teaches in its entirety. And in its entirety, the Scripture teaches about women, about Deborah who was a judge and a prophetess (Judges 4—5). Miriam was a prophetess, too (Exod 15:20). She seems also to have been a teacher.

Women also wrote some of the Scripture. What they said by the Holy Ghost was copied down, and is now in Scripture (Exod 15:1–21, Judg 5:1–31, 1 Sam 2:1–10, Prov 31:1–31, Luke 1:46–55).

So, to repeat myself, women have always been in the throng of the children of God as teachers, leaders, administrators, and prophets. But they have never been priests. God gave this task to men (Gen 2:15–17), and may God also give men the strength and wisdom to study and speak his Word and to divide his sacraments rightly.

The word "law" in the Scriptures

MY GOAL HERE IS only to discuss definitions. I want to clarify what we sometimes mean when we speak of "the law." I also want to clarify how the Scriptures use this term. Luther has already discussed all these ideas in many places and I refer you to his writings for help.

The "law" can be thought of in the theological, or spiritual-demand sense. When I speak of it this way, I try to say not "the law," but "the law with its wrath and demands." This is how Paul speaks of the law when he says "now the law works wrath" (Rom 4:15; cf. Rom 2:5–6). Those people on this earth who are not living under grace are living under the law. They are under the wrath of God.

> Now we know that what things soever the law saith, it saith to them who are under the law, that every mouth may be stopped, and all the world may become guilty before God. Therefore by the deeds of the law there shall no flesh be justified in his sight; for by the law is the knowledge of sin (Rom 3:19–20).

Also it is written: "Then the anger of the Lord and his jealousy shall smoke against that man, and all the curses that are written in this book shall lie upon him, and the Lord shall blot out his name from under heaven" (Deut 29:20). Notice that in this text, a writing is mentioned. This, we could say, in one sense, means the books of Moses. But as we will discuss below, if we speak of "the law" in the theological sense meaning "the law with all its curses and wrath" and think it means "all that is written in the books of Moses," we err. For not all the things that are written in the books of Moses are only the law with its curses and wrath. Indeed, it is a mistake to think one section of text is "law" and another section of text is "gospel," because both are meant in every text, and each heart will hear them as what God has prepared that heart to hear them as.

We know that the promises of mercy and grace in Jesus Christ are set forth beautifully in the books of Moses. Luther taught in his commentary on Deuteronomy that Moses taught Christ to the people. And we know he did. After he taught the wrath of the law, for example, at Mount Sinai, with many visible signs and wonders (Exod 19), Moses taught of love (Exod 21) and of the forgiveness of sins (Exod 24, cf. Heb 12:24). Thus, we err if we say that the five books of Moses contain only a teaching of the law with all its curses.

Jesus died to redeem us from the wrath of the law (Gal 3:13, cf. 1 Pet 1:18). When we say this, we mean Jesus died to redeem us from the law and all its demands and curses. We read in the Bible of this in many places. For example, Moses says he prayed to the Lord saying: "O Lord God destroy not thy people and thine inheritance, which thou hast redeemed through thy greatness, which thou hast brought forth out of Egypt with a mighty hand" (Deut 9:26). In the Psalms we sing: "Remember thy congregation, which thou hast purchased of old; the rod of thine inheritance, which thou hast redeemed; this mount Zion, wherein thou hast dwelt" (Ps 74:2). And: "In all their affliction he was afflicted, and the angel of his presence saved them. In his love and in his pity he redeemed them; and he bare them, and carried them all the days of old" (Isa 63:9). There was the strong one, which is sin and death, whose power was broken by the victory of the Lord Christ: "For the Lord hath redeemed Jacob, and ransomed him from the hand of him that was stronger than he" (Jer 31:11). Also: "Christ hath redeemed us from the curse of the law, being made a curse for us: for it is written: 'Cursed is every one that hangeth on a tree'" (Gal 3:13). And we sing of this redeeming to Christ, saying: "Thou art worthy to take the book, and to open the seals thereof, for thou wast slain, and hast redeemed us to God by thy blood out of every kindred, and tongue, and people, and nation" (Rev 5:9). Christ came to redeem us, or rescue us from under the curse of the law: "To redeem them that were under the law, that we might receive the adoption of sons" (Gal 4:5). Daniel writes of Christ's work of redemption and forgiveness of sins:

> Seventy weeks are determined upon thy people and upon thy holy city, to finish the transgression, and to make an end of sins, and to make reconciliation for iniquity, and to bring in everlasting righteousness, and to seal up the vision and prophecy, and to anoint the most Holy (Dan 9:24).

Jesus spoke of himself: "For this is my blood of the new testament, which is shed for many for the remission of sins" (Matt 26:28). And in Titus we read that Christ "gave himself for us, that he might redeem us from all iniquity" (Titus 2:14).

Those who are not redeemed by Christ, and do not have his Spirit, are still under the curse of the law. The preaching of the law with all its wrath and curses sounds like and continues to be a demanding and terrible law: "By the law is the knowledge of sin" (Rom 3:10). As we learn in Scriptures: "For as many as are of the works of the law are under the curse; for it is written, 'Cursed is every one that continueth not in all things which are written in the book of the law to do them'" (Gal 3:10).

The word "law," taken in the sense of "the law with all its curses and wrath," is often paralleled with "commandment" in the Scripture. Paul uses it like this often. So does John. "Commandment" thus often means "the law with all its curses and wrath." This is what is shown in Hebrews 12:18–21. Also 2 Corinthians 3:9–13. There the law with all its curses and wrath is called "the ministry of condemnation." For the law is our schoolmaster, to scare us and whip us so that we despair of ourselves and turn to Christ (Num 21:7).

Above we stated that we err if we say that the five books of the Bible, the books of Moses, contain only a teaching of the law with all its curses. Sometimes people can be led to think the books of Moses contain only the law with all its curses because of the way the word "law" is used. Someone can be speaking of "Moses," and they mean the law with all its curses. But someone could also be saying "law" meaning only "the teachings of Moses," or "the first five books of the Bible," commonly referred to as "the books of Moses." For example: "And it came to pass, when the king had heard the words of the book of the law, that he rent his clothes" (2 Kgs 22:11). At the point in time this was written, the "book of the law" simply meant the Bible, which at that time was the first five books only, which are the books of Moses. Jehoshaphat in his time sent out teachers with the Bible, and this was the Bible they had: "And they taught in Judah, and had the book of the law of the Lord with them, and went about throughout all the cities of Judah, and taught the people" (2 Chr 17:9). The book of the law of the Lord was simply Genesis through Deuteronomy. This is what "law" means in this passage of Joshua: "And [Joshua] wrote there upon the stones a copy of the law of Moses, which he wrote in the presence of the children of Israel" and "he read all the words of the law, the blessings and the cursings, according to all that is written in the book of the law" (Josh 8:32, 34). The "law" meant simply the first five books of Moses in this case. This was true also in the time of Nehemiah when the people gathered together and, "they spake unto Ezra the scribe to bring the book of the law of Moses, which the Lord had commanded to Israel" (Neh 8:1). Jesus, in his time, named the Bible as containing "the Law, the Prophets, and the Psalms" (Luke 24:44).

So we see that the word "law" in Scripture does not always mean "the law with all its curses and wrath." The word "law" in the Scripture can mean just the first five books of the Bible. The word can also simply mean "teachings," or "teaching."

Have mercy on me

WHAT DO I DO when I am told by those who I hold as ministers of Christ on earth that I am in a wrong spiritual state, that I am not living of grace? It is almost worse than being one of the ungodly. For if I had been one of the heathen, I could have repented. But how can one repent when one is already a Christian? When one has repented of unbelief and all sin, and all sin is already forgiven, drowned in the sea of mercy, what else is there to repent of?

The same situation is true when a Christian gets "bound" by Christians. The definition of a heathen is one who is bound. So how can someone be a Christian and bound? It is not possible. And if one is in a wrong spirit, then one must not be in the Holy Spirit. Therefore one is in the spirit of falsehood, and is an infidel. So how can someone have the Holy Spirit and at the same time a wrong spirit? It is not possible.

I remember clinging to Christ. I remember: "For the law of the Spirit of life in Christ Jesus hath made me free from the law of sin and death" (Rom 8:2). I remember: "As the truth of Christ is in me, no man shall stop me of this boasting in the regions of Achaia" (2 Cor 11:10). I remember: "Christ liveth in me" (Gal 2:20). I knew that if Christ lived in me, then I would be seen through Christ by God. And my Father judges me according to Christ's merits, not mine. But that was all I had, these assurances and promises of God: "For we which live are always delivered unto death for Jesus' sake, that the life also of Jesus might be made manifest in our mortal flesh" (2 Cor 4:11).

This is a common remembrance in the psalms, that we are to be judged by the perfection that is in us, that is, Christ: "Judge me, O Lord, according to my righteousness, and according to my perfection that is in me" (Ps 7:8). The children of God are often called "the perfect" in the Bible, because Christ's perfect righteousness is ours, and it is through that righteousness that we are judged, and we also judge the other children of God through that righteousness—they find grace in our sight, as they have in the eyes of God (Gen 17:1, 2 Sam 22:33, Matt 5:48, 19:21, 1 Cor 2:6, Phil 3:15).

I, being completely blind, see perfectly, through the Spirit of God. But of myself I am completely blind: "And, behold, two blind men sitting by the way side, when they heard that Jesus passed by, cried out, saying, 'Have mercy on us, O Lord, thou Son of David'" (Matt 20:30). As Isaiah said: "Who is blind, but my servant? Or deaf, as my messenger that I sent? Who is blind as he that is perfect, and blind as the Lord's servant?" (42:19). But if I said that I see of myself, of my own power, then I would be blind, and my sin would remain (John 9).

O Son of David, have mercy on me. For "he is not ashamed to call them brethren" (Heb 2:11). And so I am very bold: "Great is my boldness of speech towards you" (2 Cor 7:4). For in Christ "we have boldness and access with confidence by the faith of him" (Eph 3:12).

Ministers gone astray

IT IS TRUE THAT we should obey those who have the rule over us (Heb 13:17). But not if they have gone astray, if they are "contrary to the doctrine which ye have learned" (Rom 16:17). Because leaders and ministers can go astray (Mal 1:6). They can be "departed out of the way" and cause many to stumble at the teachings of God and corrupt the covenant of Levi (Mal 2:8). This is why we must not believe every spirit, "but try the spirits whether they are of God; because many false prophets are gone out into the world" (1 John 4:1).

Jeremiah preached against false prophets and evil priests (Jer 5:30–31, 23:15). So did Ezekiel. He said that the priests "have put no difference between the holy and profane" (Ezek 22:26). Hosea also preached against priests who had gone astray (Hos 4:6, 5:1–2). In his day some of the priests were soul-murderers and committed lewdness (Hos 6:9). Many also went astray during the time of Zephaniah, and some were priests, and some were prophets (Zeph 3:3–4). Isaiah talked about the tables of vomit that the priests had (Isa 28:8).

Paul wrote to Timothy about those who were wrongly teaching in his day (1 Tim 1:4–7). He wrote that some departed from the faith and began "speaking lies in hypocrisy" (1 Tim 4:2). Paul warned about wolves, saying: "Also of your own selves shall men arise, speaking perverse things, to draw away disciples after them" (Acts 20:30). People can fall away and be like Jannes and Jambres, who "withstood Moses"; these people "resist the truth" and are "men of corrupt minds, reprobate concerning the faith" (2 Tim 3:8). But "their folly shall be manifest to all men" (2 Tim 3:9). Peter warns us that just as in the time of the Old Testament there were false prophets among the people, they will also be among us who secretly "shall bring in damnable heresies" (2 Pet 2:1). So let us be aware that there are such things as "false apostles, deceitful workers" who transform themselves into the apostles of Christ (2 Cor 11:13). We have to be careful to only obey those who are speaking the pure Word, for "if they speak not according to this word, it is because there is no light in them" (Isa 8:20). God will help us even in this.

The church law of Christ

WHAT THE CHURCH LAW of Christ says should happen when someone falls, we also find happening in the Scriptures. For the church law of Christ is that if one is trespassed against by another, he is to go visit with the one who offended him alone: "Debate your matter with your neighbor himself, and discover not a secret to another" (Prov 25:9). The one who knows about the sin is not to first go tell another, but he is to go to the offending one as his equal. He is to go without any friends or supporters, but so that it is only these two: the one who has done the wrong, or is perceived such, and the one who is wrong, or is perceiving a wrong. This is what Jesus taught: "And also, if your brother trespasses against you, go and tell him his fault between you and him alone; if he hears you, you have gained your brother" (Matt 18:15). Sometimes two people feel as if they are very piously and in the right spirit discussing the matters of a third person. But they ought not to feel this way. Rather, one of them alone should go first and directly to that other person about whom there is some kind of question or offense. Jesus teaches: "Take heed to yourselves: if your brother trespasses against you, rebuke him; and if he repents, forgive him" (Luke 17:3). Often two individuals speaking together ends the matter. James writes: "Brethren, if any of you do err from the truth, and one convert him, let him know, that he which converteth the sinner from the error of his way shall save a soul from death, and shall hide a multitude of sins" (5:19–20).

Then, if the person who has offended, whose soul needs care, does not hear in the one-on-one conversation, a few others are to be brought. As it is written: "But if he will not hear you, then take with you one or two more, that in the mouth of two or three witnesses every word may be established" (Matt 18:16). And finally: "And if he neglects to hear them, tell it to the church; but if he neglects to hear the church, let him be to you as a heathen man and a publican" (Matt 18:17).

Sometimes, of course, someone doesn't even need to take the first step. He can just ponder a matter that seems to be a difficulty between himself and another, and realize that there is no soul care involved, it is just a little fault he perceived, perhaps in his own mind, and he forgives the other person without ever speaking to him. We are duty bound to have forgiving, Christ-like minds towards the others. If we do not forgive from the heart, the consequences are dire: "So likewise shall my heavenly Father do also to you, if you from your hearts do not forgive every one his brother their trespasses" (Matt 18:35). Paul says to the Corinthians that the brothers and sisters ought not battle over matters, but rather, that one should immediately give in to the other, and let go of a matter, even if it is his own pride, or something of his, that has been damaged: "Now therefore there is utterly a fault among you, because ye go to law one with another. Why do ye not rather take wrong? Why do ye not rather suffer yourselves to be defrauded?" (1 Cor 6:7). We are to immediately forgive, and be "forbearing one another, and forgiving one another, if any man have a quarrel against any; even as Christ forgave you, so also do ye" (Col 3:13). Jesus exhorted: "Agree with thine adversary quickly, whiles thou art in the way with him; lest at any time the adversary deliver thee to the judge, and the judge deliver thee to the officer, and thou be cast into prison" (Matt 5:25).

It is deep love to go speak one-on-one and face-to-face. This is what is written in Scriptures: "Thou shalt not hate thy brother in thine heart; thou shalt in any wise rebuke thy neighbor, and not suffer sin upon him" (Lev 19:17). Paul did this to Peter, as he said: "But when Peter had come to Antioch, I withstood him to the face, because he was to be blamed" (Gal 2:11). And David rebuked Nathan to his face (2 Sam 12:13). David's brothers, who followed Saul, did not do this. They came as a group and accused David.

And they did not accuse him of sin, rather, they accused him of being a sinner (1 Sam 17:28). They cruelly interpreted his actions, which were very innocent, which is also what Eli did to Hannah (1 Sam 1:14). And when Korah and his followers had a concern about something Moses and Aaron were doing wrong, they came as a group and accused them:

> And they rose up before Moses, with certain of the children of Israel, two hundred and fifty princes of the assembly, famous in the congregation, men of renown. And they gathered themselves together against Moses and against Aaron, and said unto them: "Ye take too much upon you, seeing all the congregation are holy, every one of them, and the Lord is among them; wherefore then lift ye up yourselves above the congregation of the Lord?" (Num 16:2–3).

Those who wanted to accuse the builders in Jerusalem did not go visit with them, rather, they stirred up others against them, including the authorities (Ezra 4:1–6). And Balak, the king of the Moabites, also did not openly and publicly try to dispute about matters of soul; rather, he hired Balaam to curse the people (Num 22:1–6).

As the church law of Christ states, after a one-on-one discussion fails, then one or two are to be taken to discuss a matter of soul care. But then, if that fails, the congregation is turned to: "Them that sin rebuke before all, that others also may fear" (1 Tim 5:20). All are to hear, and learn, because we are all subject to sin, and equally and commonly (1 Cor 10:13, Jas 5:10). We should endeavor to do what is good, what builds up (Rom 14:19).

As Korah and those brothers of Saul who accused David, those called "Pharisees" in the gospels did not go to Jesus. They did not go to discuss between him and them alone if they saw a need for soul care, or if they were feeling as if there was wrong teaching going on. Neither did the Pharisees openly and publicly preach before all the people trying to correct false teachings, as Jesus did (Matt 5—7). Rather they came in groups to accuse Jesus (Ps 2:2, 56:6, 59:3, 71:10, Matt 27:1, Mark 12:13, Luke 11:54, 20:20, John 8:6, cf. Dan 6:4). They also accused him to the authorities (Luke 23:2).

Compassion on heretics

IT IS WRITTEN ABOUT a situation with some who opposed the prophet of God, Jeremiah, that they were cruel:

> Then said they, come, and let us devise devices against Jeremiah, for "the law shall not perish from the priest, nor counsel from the wise, nor the word from the prophet." Come and let us smite him with the tongue, and let us not give heed to any of his words (Jer 18:18).

Note here about heretics and false teachers that they quote Scripture, and know right doctrine. So what they say, part of it is true. There is much partial following of God going on at the time before a heresy, as we see in Numbers 14. God says of Caleb in Numbers 14:24: "He has followed me fully." In other words, some are following God but only partially, as in the time of Elijah (1 Kgs 18:21). But Caleb followed completely, or fully. He was as Paul. For Paul says to the elders of the people in Ephesus, he kept back nothing that was profitable for the people (Acts 20:20). Some preachers say much, even a great deal, of the Word of God, but they hold back just some of it, things that people really need to hear, words of rebuke, or help, or comfort. Caleb did not do this, because it says in that same place in Numbers, he had the Spirit.

Note second in this text above from Jeremiah that heretics and false teachers smite with the tongue. They go after those children of God who teach rightly. It gets so bad for those who teach the Word rightly during times of spiritual storms that the poor teachers of God's Word say with Jeremiah: "I will not make mention of him, nor speak any more in his name." But God compels them by his Spirit in them. So they say: "But his Word was in mine heart as a burning fire shut up in my bones, and I was weary with holding back, and I could not" (Jer 20:9).

And note thirdly that the false teachers say "his words"—in other words, they think that those who are speaking and teaching by the Spirit are acting and speaking and teaching according to their own minds, not the mind of God. False teachers think according to the flesh and wisdom of man. They don't recognize the Spirit. This is what Moses lamented about Korah, saying: "Hereby ye shall know that the Lord hath sent me to do all these works; for I have not done them of mine own mind" (Num 16:28).

Let us be watchful in these things, and have compassion on false teachers, Pharisees and scribes, and heretics, and so we can say truly and confidently as Jeremiah to God: "Remember that I stood before thee to speak good for them, and to turn away thy wrath from them" (Jer 18:20). For as Jeremiah continues in that same place, there comes a time when God will no longer call out and beseech—the time of Sodom and Gomorrah comes, the time of God's anger after long forbearance, and the Spirit says:

> Therefore deliver up their children to the famine, and pour out their blood by the force of the sword; and let their wives be bereaved of their children, and be widows; and let their men be put to death; let their young men be slain by the sword in battle. Let a cry be heard from their houses, when thou shalt bring a troop suddenly upon them. For they have digged a pit to take me, and hid snares for my feet. Yet, Lord, thou knowest all their counsel against me to slay me; forgive not their iniquity, neither blot out their sin from thy sight, but let them be overthrown before thee; deal thus with them in the time of thine anger (Jer 18:21–23).

The imagination

WHAT WOULD BE A better way to translate the word that is translated "imagination" in Genesis 6:5? For it says that "every imagination of the thoughts of [man's] heart was only evil continually." And in Genesis 8:21 it is repeated: "For the imagination of man's heart is evil from his youth." Should it be better translated every "purpose," or every "thought formed"?

Jeremiah quotes this text from Moses more than once, but there the word that is also translated "imagination" in English is different in the original language. It means "stubbornness," or "twistedness." Jeremiah 7:24 says: "But they hearkened not, nor inclined their ear, but walked in the counsels and in the imagination of their evil heart, and went backward, and not forward." And Jeremiah 9:14 says that the people "have walked after the imagination of their own heart, and after Baalim, which their fathers taught them."

When Mary sings her song of praise in the first chapter of Luke, she says: "He hath shewed strength with his arm; he hath scattered the proud in the imagination of their hearts" (Luke 1:51). This also refers to the first book of Moses. The Greek word that is translated "imagination" simply means "mind," or "understanding."

So the disposition, or purposes, or understandings of our mind are always evil continually. What our own hearts devise is always only evil. That is why when there come controversies or disagreements among us, we must never think: "Well, I am in the right and the others are in the wrong." For we are all, always, completely wrong. But Christ is in us (Gal 2:20, John 14:20), by his Spirit, and he is always right. He gives us understanding (Ps 119:99). And sometimes, in spite of our flesh, he speaks through us—his voice and message come out, instead of our own. Others who have the Spirit recognize it. And this is right, and all who oppose this teaching voice of Christ are wrong. As it is written: "Now then we are ambassadors for Christ, as though God did beseech you by us: we pray you in Christ's stead, be ye reconciled to God" (2 Cor 5:20).

Sadly, our flesh is always so strong! And therefore the Spirit of Christ in us is seldom heard. Instead, the flesh and the evil imaginations of our own heart speak. May God help us!

Your sin will find you out

GOD VISITS PEOPLE'S SINS back on them. In other words, it is not so much that God *punishes* people for the sins that they commit. It's more that God *visits* people's sins upon them. In other words, sin carries in it its own punishment and consequence. The Bible relates that we can be sure that our sin will find us out (Num 32:23).

So the word translated "visit" is well-translated, and it is better to translate that Hebrew word "visit" than "punish." For the lake of fire was not created for man, but for the devil and his angels (Matt 25:41). But the devil has deceived the whole world (Rev 12:9). He has led the lost ones captive at his will (2 Tim 2:26; Col 1:13).

And God, mercifully, has saved us from the devil and has visited on us less than our iniquities have deserved. But if we rebel, the land of the saints of God will reject us: "That the land spew you not out also, when ye defile it, as it spewed out the nations that were before you" (Lev 18:28). As it is written: "For a voice of wailing is heard out of Zion: 'How are we plundered! We are greatly shamed, because we have forsaken the land, because our dwellings have cast us out'" (Jer 9:19).

So when we sin, we should confess it, and not blame others, and we should know that "thy way and thy doings have provided these things unto thee" (Jer 4:18). As it is also written to us: "Your iniquities have thrust these things away from you, and your sins have withheld good from you" (Jer 5:25). God warns us:

> And go not after other gods to serve them, and to worship them, and provoke me not to anger with the works of your hands; and I will do you no hurt. Yet ye have not

hearkened unto me, saith the Lord; that ye might provoke me to anger with the works of your hands to your own hurt (Jer 25:6–7).

For if we do the works of our own hands rather than God's will, it will surely be said of us: "Hear, O earth! Behold, I will bring evil upon this people, even the fruit of their thoughts, because they have not hearkened unto my words, nor to my law, but rejected it" (Jer 6:19). For if we sin and do not repent, eventually faith is lost, we are left under the wrath of God. And if we live under the law we are cursed and judged by its severity. We get left to our own devices, with no Spirit to stop us (Ps 81:12). And then there is nothing left to us but wrath. God says: "Now is the end come upon thee, and I will send mine anger upon thee, and will judge thee according to thy ways, and I will recompense upon thee all thine abominations" (Ezek 7:3). Curses fall on us, curses that grace had been holding back (Deut 28:45).

May we not go the way of Sodom! "The shew of their countenance doth witness against them. And they declare their sin as Sodom, they hide it not. Woe unto their soul! For they have rewarded evil unto themselves" (Isa 3:9). God will help us even in this.

Thanks and praise

JUST IMAGINE IF, AS a parent, you got a list of wants, of needs, from your child. The list asks for many things—it is a confession that that child does not have things, and needs them. In reading such a letter, would you feel praised? Would you feel thanked?

This is what God says he does. For example, we read in a song: "And call upon me in the day of trouble. I will deliver thee, and thou shalt glorify me" (Ps 50:15). In other words, God is praised and thanked most when we ask him for things, when we ask him for his blessing. By this, his reputation is preserved—he is held up as how he wants to be held up and remembered: as the one who redeems, who delivers, who helps. This is his highest praise. He is like a king among kings. The other kings have reputations of fear and terror. God has a reputation of mercy towards the penitent.

The word often translated "praise" in the psalms and elsewhere in the Old Testament can also be translated "confession." So "confessing-praiser" would be a good translation of the word. The name "Judah" comes from this word. Thus, the name Judah means "confessing-praiser," or something to that effect. The tribe of Judah is the tribe that Christ came from. Christ is praised by our confession and absolution. It is written: "He that covereth his sins shall not prosper, but whoso confesseth and forsaketh them shall have mercy" (Prov 28:13). Also:

> If they shall confess their iniquity, and the iniquity of their fathers, with their trespass which they trespassed against me, and that also they have walked contrary unto me; and that I also have walked contrary unto them, and

have brought them into the land of their enemies; if then their uncircumcised hearts be humbled, and they then accept of the punishment of their iniquity. Then will I remember my covenant with Jacob, and also my covenant with Isaac, and also my covenant with Abraham will I remember; and I will remember the land (Lev 26:40–42).

The text feeds

DREAMS AND OTHER LANGUAGES are to be interpreted. This is how we think of them, naturally. But why do we always say the Bible is to be "interpreted"? It's very rare for the Bible to use this term in reference to itself. It is used only in Peter where the Greek word that the KJV translates "interpretation" is something like "loosening," or "explanation," or "application" (2 Pet 1:20).

The Bible is a nourisher. It feeds. The text is to be taught. And we are to be taught by it, and fed by it. It is prophecy and sermon and poetry. "And I will set up shepherds over them which shall feed them" (Jer 23:4). The Bible texts are enlighteners, warners. So when we approach a text, we do better to think of it as something that will feed us, that will rebuke us or remind us of things we already know, rather than approach the text as almost as if it is some mathematical problem to be solved, to be interpreted. For where in the Bible is God compared to a mathematician? Is he not a Shepherd, a gardener, a Father, a good King? "For whatsoever things were written aforetime were written for our learning, that we through patience and comfort of the Scriptures might have hope" (Rom 15:4).

We can always get some nourishment from every text, even if we don't "interpret" it the right way—even if we don't "get" it or "understand" it perfectly. Every text will feed and remind in some way. Even genealogies. For even genealogies remind us that Christ was born of a human being, of the flesh, and of a certain tribe and at a certain time, and that yet he was true God. But he knows how to bear with our weaknesses and carry us. And one way he does this is by the written Word, which is food, and good medicine, and sweet manna that tastes of heavenly delights.

The text is a provider of provisions for a journey. It is our songbook to sing. It is our remembrancer. It is our letter from our Father that we read and re-read, to keep always in mind his comfort and promises to us. And the text is also Christ's final will and testament. It is a legal document of promise, which cannot be revoked. And we know:

> He is the mediator of the new testament, that by means of death, for the redemption of the transgressions that were under the first testament, they which are called might receive the promise of eternal inheritance. For where a testament is, there must also of necessity be the death of the testator. For a testament is of force after men are dead; otherwise it is of no strength at all while the testator liveth (Heb 9:15–17).

He wrote this testament to us, and sealed it with his own blood. The text of the Bible works like an engagement ring works to a married or engaged person. The text of the Bible is a constant renewal of God's vows of grace to us. We should learn it, remember it, care for it, and hold it as such.

Makeup and earrings

THE BIBLE DOESN'T MENTION much about makeup except to mention that Jezebel put it on once (2 Kgs 9:30). But earrings get mentioned quite often. Rebekah wore earrings in Genesis 24:47 (however, it could have been a nose ring). The people took earrings out of their ears, along with other items of gold, to give to Aaron to make the golden calf (Exod 32:2–3). The kingdom of God, in Ezekiel 16, is compared to a beautiful woman, and among her adornments are earrings. Jewels and earrings are also mentioned in the lesson using a female in Hosea 2. In Isaiah 3, the proud are discussed, pictured as a vain woman, and earrings are mentioned here as well.

The believers at the end of the book of Job gave earrings of gold as part of a blessing (Job 42:11–12). And Proverbs 25:12 says: "As an earring of gold, and an ornament of fine gold, so is a wise reprover upon an obedient ear" (Prov 25:12).

So then, how are we to understand the use of makeup and earrings? For earrings are something mentioned in good ways and bad ways in the Bible. Romans 14 says we are not to despise people who understand certain matters differently from us. We are not to judge people in these adornment matters, but we are to ask ourselves before we put on the earrings and before we talk to someone else about it, am I walking charitably? Am I following after the things which make for peace and the things which can edify when I do this (Rom 14:19)?

In 1 Corinthians 8 the same matter is spoken of. If we say that we love God, and hate our neighbor, we don't love God. We are not to put a stumblingblock before our brother. "When ye sin so against the brethren and wound their weak conscience, ye sin against Christ" (1 Cor 8:12).

Let us not love the world. Let us not love the things that are in the world. Let us not be vain. And let us love our neighbors. For everything we do, we actually do not do for ourselves, but for our brothers and sisters. As it is written: "No man liveth or dieth to himself" (Rom 14:7).

The end of the book of Judges

IF YOU GET TEN people in a room, and have them read the last few chapters of the book of Judges, the response to the text that you get from them tells you all you need to know about what this text "means." For the law is to reveal sin. This text reveals sin. Not by what is in the text, but by the responses that people have to the text. As Luther noticed, the rabbis in their commentaries on Moses revealed their base minds everywhere by their responses to the text. In other words, we may be in doubt as to what Moses was up to in any given text, but we're very clear on what those who respond to him are up to, by how they respond to the text—and this, in the end, is a lot of what Moses is up to: to reveal sin.

Let's go back to our ten people in the room reading this text from Judges. I submit to you (because I have seen it) that if one of the ten has a clean conscience, a pure heart, he will very likely be perplexed by this text. That is likely to be his first reaction, just as it probably would be to the two closely related texts, Genesis 19 and Genesis 34. But, and this is key, the one with the pure heart would refuse to do what many others, who have bad consciences, will do, which is to blame God or to imply that God is to be blamed, that he promotes violence, hurting of women, genocide and other such things. Our pure-hearted one, if told by someone else that the text is awful, that it promotes wickedness, will probably very meekly say, "I just don't think so." And if pressed and asked, "Well then what is this text up to?" he might simply confess the truth, that he doesn't know.

Again, a pure-hearted one will not ascribe evil to God. He will think that the fault is in himself, the darkness is his own. He will think that the reason he doesn't understand the text is because he is sinful and wretched.

Notice, our pure-hearted one has comprehended the first task of this text, which is to reveal the thoughts and intents of the hearts of men. For this is what the Word of God does: "Then Jael Heber's wife took a nail of the tent, and took a hammer in her hand, and went softly unto him, and smote the nail into his temples, and fastened it into the ground. For he was fast asleep and weary. So he died" (Judg 4:21). And: "'Is not my word like as a fire?' saith the Lord; 'and like a hammer that breaketh the rock in pieces?'" (Jer 23:29).

The one with a bad conscience who criticizes God for writing such an awful text is saying nothing about what the end of the book of Judges teaches. He is simply saying: if I would have written this, here is what I would have been intending: wickedness. Which tells us a great deal about him, but nothing about the end of the book of Judges.

To never have forgiveness

THE BIBLE SAYS: "BUT he that shall blaspheme against the Holy Ghost hath never forgiveness, but is in danger of eternal damnation" (Mark 3:29). It is a text often inquired into. People, especially young people, wonder what it means. They are aware that God is telling them that there is a possibility that exists, which is the possibility that we would abide outside of the grace of God, outside of the forgiveness of God, and that additionally, we would be in such a condition that we would never be able to get back into grace—we would have forgiveness never. Now, the text wishes to let us know that such a possibility exists. We know Esau was in such a state. But the text does not give us permission to decide whether another person is in that state or not. The text is for us, for me, to look into my own matters, not those of another. The text wishes to warn me, me personally, so that I would watch out for my own self, that I would not fall into this state of blasphemy against the Holy Ghost.

Friends! Look at what the very next verse informs us. It says: "Because they said, he hath an unclean spirit" (Mark 3:30). In other words, blasphemy against the Holy Ghost, and thus having forgiveness never, is connected with judging—it is judging the other children of God, and saying of them, "he hath a devil."

You see the irony—those who judge other children of God and call them devils or imply that the devil is pretty much in charge of them, they lack charity and forgiveness. And thus they put themselves at risk, if they persist in their pernicious ways, of being outside of grace and never being able to get back in.

So let us not be, as the Bible says, self-willed. And let us be very afraid to "speak evil of dignities" (2 Pet 2:10)—which means, to speak evil things about other children of God. Or else it means not to speak evil of glories, that is, to despise the pleasant land (Ps 106:24).

Jacob and Laban and Esau

LET US LOOK AT the way of grace and peace by studying part of the story of Jacob. Jacob was blessed: "And God Almighty bless you, and make you fruitful, and multiply you, that you may be an assembly of people" (Gen 28:3). And Jacob, because of the grace of God in his heart, wanted to follow the Lord. Jacob vowed a vow after he had seen the angels ascending and descending to the earth: "If God will be with me, and will keep me in this way that I go . . ." (Gen 28:20).

Because he had a heart of faith, Jacob's first inquiry about people when he met them was whether they were in the peace of God. He understood that the most important concern a man should have is the condition of his soul. Is there the peace of God in the heart? After Jacob first came to Haran he asked the shepherds at the well about Laban. He asked them: "Is there peace to Laban?" (Gen 29:6). As the story of Jacob and Laban shows, Laban, over time, lost the peace of God. But at first Laban did have peace. When Jacob fled from his brother Esau, Jacob went to Laban's. There Jacob began his work by watering the flock of Laban, his mother's brother (Gen 29:10). This is the service of love that Jacob began with. As it is written: "Follow peace with all men, and holiness, without which no man shall see the Lord" (Heb 12:14). So Jacob's intentions were peace and holiness, the fruits of the Holy Ghost—kindness, grace, giving.

Laban spoke the words of faith and kindness and friendliness, too. He told Jacob: "Surely you are my bone and my flesh" (Gen 29:11). He recognized that they were of the same body. As

Paul writes: "So we, being many, are one body in Christ, and every one members one of another" (Rom 12:5). Jacob and Laban were brothers in faith at this time. Laban called Jacob his brother (Gen 29:15), just as Jacob had called Laban's shepherds his brothers (Gen 29:4).

Jacob's heart of faith is seen in his heart of service. Jacob served Laban (Gen 30:26). He did as the Scriptures taught—that we serve one another in love: "Be slaves to one another in love" (Gal 5:13). This is the fulfilling of the law (Gal 5:14), that we love our neighbor. And the law is fulfilled through faith in the promises of God.

Paul writes: "Be slaves to one another in love" (Gal 5:13). When Paul writes this, he has specific activities in mind that he opposes, things that he does not wish to be among the congregation: biting and devouring one another. For this is what fulfilling the lusts of the flesh also is: going after our neighbor with bitings and devourings.

Jacob was blessed in not doing those wrongs against his neighbor, Laban. Jacob did not do wrong to Laban even though we see as time went by that Laban's heart changed. We might say that at first it was easy for Jacob to be serving Laban, but towards the end it got more and more difficult because Laban's heart changed completely during that time period.

Envy was surely one of the reasons. God blessed Jacob, and even Laban received increase because of this blessing (Gen 30:30). Laban was envious. But why was Jacob so blessed? Because he remained in the Spirit. Therefore his fruits were seen. The names of his children show this. One is "a son," which pictures the firstborn son the Lord Jesus by faith. And "hearing" because Jacob heard the Word, and God also heard his prayers. Jacob remained in watchful prayer. Also "joined"—Jacob remained joined to the congregation, which is the body of Christ. And "praise"—Jacob confessed his sins and believed them forgiven, and this was praise of God (Ps 50:14–15). Jacob also praised the Christ, and not himself, and walked along in that humility and meekness that is Christ's (Gen 29:32–35).

Many other fruits of faith also showed in Jacob's life (Gen 30:1–22). And Jacob was blessed even though Laban opposed him and changed his wages. Jacob went out of his way to give the benefit of the doubt to Laban (Gen 30:33), and bore any loss himself, as Christ teaches to do in the Sermon on the Mount (Matt 5:39–42). This is what we are instructed to do by God: "Yea, all of you be subject one to another, and be clothed with humility" (1 Pet 5:5). Also: "Be kindly affectioned one to another with brotherly love; in honor preferring one another" (Rom 12:10). It is also written that we ought to be submitting ourselves "one to another in the fear of God" (Eph 5:21). And Paul writes to the Philippians: "Let nothing be done through strife or vainglory; but in lowliness of mind let each esteem the other better than themselves" (2:3).

But even though great brotherly love was shown to Laban by Jacob, in his heart Laban moved apart from Jacob (Gen 30:36). And Jacob showed, by what he did next, that Laban's teachings should not be given growth, but rather, Jacob's teachings, which were godly, should be nourished and given growth. And God blessed Jacob even more (Gen 30:37–43).

It came out more into the open eventually, the separation that existed between Jacob and Laban. Their conditions of heart, which previously had been the same, were now different. The same was true of Laban's sons, who spoke enviously of Jacob (Gen 31:1).

And the condition of heart was in some way revealed on Laban's face, because Jacob noticed that "it was not towards him as before" (Gen 31:2). Jacob may not have said anything to Laban about this. But we know he kept going on teaching and helping and serving Laban no matter what, just as he was supposed to.

What was this face, or countenance, of Laban? It means Laban no longer looked at Jacob through grace. This is how the Bible teaches that we, as brothers and sisters of Jesus Christ, ought to look at one another: through grace. That is, we do not look at each other according to faults and sins, character deficiencies, or remembrances of past sins, but rather, we look on each other as pardoned through the grace of God, as clothed in the beauty of Christ's own righteousness.

This is what the Bible teaches us. For example, looking at someone with grace is coupled with being overflowingly merciful in Genesis 19:19. And in 1 Samuel 20:3, David testifies to Jonathan that Jonathan looks at David through grace: "I have found grace in thine eyes," he says. Jesus says in Luke 6:36: "Be ye therefore merciful, as your Father also is merciful." And in Matthew it is said of Jesus how he looked at people: "But when he saw the multitudes he was moved with compassion on them, because they fainted, and were scattered abroad, as sheep having no shepherd" (Matt 9:36, cf. Matt 14:14). And Jesus even called the disciples and told them: "I have compassion on the multitude" (Matt 15:32).

The Good Samaritan in Jesus' parable saw a man half dead on the roadside and the Bible says: "When he saw him, he had compassion on him" (Luke 10:33). Peter exhorts us to be compassionate and merciful and loving (1 Pet 3:8).

Laban failed from grace, and the fruit of this showed in his life. He was no longer always wishing grace on the other, as the apostles did so many times (Acts 15:40, Rom 1:7, 16:20, 24, 1 Cor 1:3, 16:23, 2 Cor 1:2, 13:14, Gal 1:3, 6:18, Eph 1:2, 6:24, Phil 1:2, 4:23, Col 1:2, 4:18, 1 Thess 1:1, 5:28, 2 Thess 1:2, 3:18, 1 Tim 1:2, 6:21, 2 Tim 1:2, 4:22, Titus 1:4, 3:15, Plm 1:3, 25, Heb 13:25, 1 Pet 1:2, 2 Pet 1:2, 2 John 1:3, Rev 1:4, 22:21). And so Laban became deceitful and cruel in his behavior towards Jacob, although he put on a good outward show. But God saw all that Laban did to Jacob, and God was with Jacob (Gen 31:5, 12). Laban, on the other hand, had a heart that had fallen away from the living God. The Bible says that when Jacob left, Jacob stole the heart of Laban (Gen 31:20, 27). This is because Jacob either knowingly or unknowingly left with Laban's idols (Gen 31:30). Whether Jacob left with the items knowingly or unknowingly is not as important as this: Jacob had the items, but they did not possess Jacob's heart. To him it was just household stuff (Gen 30:37). If it was money, Jacob thought of it as just money, and not a god. In other words, he had it, but he didn't worship it. If it was power or pleasure, or glory, he just thought of them the way a Christian does, as things of man, things we have in this life, but not as goods or gods to be worshipped—nothing we should cling to with our heart. But these gods of this world had taken possession of Laban's heart. And so with sadness we watch him chasing after these gods—although he said he was only wishing he could greet his daughters goodbye. His heart reveals itself as concerned with these possessions of money and status when he says: "Why did you steal my gods?" (Gen 31:30). In this phrase his accusing mind is also revealed. He does not interpret actions charitably, but in the worst possible way.

After twenty years of patiently bearing with Laban, Jacob became angry and disputed with Laban. This is a sign for us how God, who is patient, and calls out lovingly, will not always do so. At some point the calling time ends, the day of visitation (Isa 55:6), as it did this time with Laban. Jacob told how matters were (Gen 31:36-42). After that, the two made a promise, for they somehow knew that from that point on they would be absent from one another (Gen 31:49; 1 John 2:19).

And Laban revealed his own wicked intentions when Laban subtly accused Jacob of wishing Laban and Laban's daughters harm and of wishing to have more wives (Gen 31:50-52). Finally the two of them sat down to eat. But they did not eat together. For the Bible says Jacob called his brothers to eat with him (Gen 31:54). And Laban was no longer of the brotherhood of faith, as he even now openly showed by his swearing an oath by the god of Nahor (Gen 31:53). Since Laban mentions the God of Abraham too, it is sure that Laban was fully convinced that he was in the right faith. He had the name of a Christian, but this was just an outward show. Paul writes:

> For he is not a Jew, which is one outwardly, neither is that circumcision, which is outward in the flesh. But he is a Jew, which is one inwardly; and whose circumcision is that of the heart in the Spirit, and not in the letter, whose praise is not of men, but of God (Rom 2:28-29).

Laban was like those of whom Jesus taught, that they are hypocrites: "Well did Isaiah prophesy of you, saying, these people draw nigh to me with their mouth, and honor me with their lips, but their heart is far from me" (Matt 15:7-8, cf. Isa 29:13). And Ezekiel writes: "For with their mouth they show much love, but their heart goes after their coveteousness" (33:31).

After this final meal, Jacob left and visited with some of the messengers of God (Gen 32:1). He sent some messengers to Esau. For Jacob was returning to the land where Esau lived, and Esau had sought to kill him. What was Jacob's attitude towards Esau in such a situation? He was very kind. He wanted to find grace in Esau's sight—he wanted there to be grace between the two of them (Gen 32:5). He wanted the first way they looked at each other after such a long time to be a look of grace, on Jacob's face, and on Esau's face. Jacob hoped when there was not even the possibility for hope (Rom 4:18). Such was his love—he prayed even when the situation with Esau's heart seemed so hopeless.

But it didn't look like the meeting was going to go well. When the messengers returned, they only said Esau was coming to meet Jacob "and there are four hundred men with him" (Gen 32:6). Jacob was afraid, and prayed to God (Gen 32:7–13).

What did Jacob do then? He was even more merciful. Because of the grace Spirit that worked in him, he did the works that faith does. He was of that spiritual Israel: "Truly God is good to Israel, even to such as are of a clean heart" (Ps 73:1). The Bible says Jacob took a grace-gift for Esau (Gen 32:13).

What was Jacob's thought at this time? The Bible tells us (Gen 32:20). He said: "I will atone for his face with the grace-gift that goes before me, and afterward I will see his face; perhaps he will accept my face [literally, *lift up/forgive my face*]." Jacob knew if Esau accepted the grace of God through the messengers Jacob sent, that then Esau and he would both be abiding in the grace of God. For Jacob himself saw God's face (Gen 32:30) and he knew that when one lived under the shining face of the grace of God, the others who also lived that way would be brothers, not in flesh and blood, but in the Spirit. "That which is born of the flesh is flesh, and that which is born of the Spirit is Spirit" (John 3:6).

Then Jacob saw Esau coming (Gen 33:1). Jacob came towards Esau in the humility of Christ (Gen 33:3; 2 Cor 10:1). Esau met Jacob kindly—perhaps the message of the graciousness of God that the messengers had brought to him had melted him a little. But when Jacob offered the gift, Esau said he had enough and refused it (Gen 33:8–9). But Jacob urged Esau again. And Esau accepted it.

Sadly, though this was Esau's outward action, he didn't go on travelling with Jacob. Esau eventually threw Jacob's yoke off his neck—it was a good yoke (Matt 11:30), but to Esau it felt evil, so he completely left. Here in Genesis 33, Esau and Jacob discussed being together, but in the end they parted. So whatever Esau meant in accepting the gift, it didn't mean that he wanted to be with Jacob as a brother in faith (Gen 33:15–17). Jacob continued on with the children, going in the footsteps of children (Gen 33:14). Esau did not. He became like those who have an outward name of being a Christian, but are not. To such ones God speaks: "Hear ye this, O house of Jacob, which are called by the name of Israel, and are come forth out of the waters of Judah, which swear by the name of the Lord, and make mention of the God of Israel, but not in truth, nor in righteousness" (Isa 46:1). Esau may have had the promise, and the sign of the promise, which in his day was circumcision, but he was not inwardly pure through grace. He was uncircumcised in heart:

> Egypt, and Judah, and Edom, and the children of Ammon, and Moab, and all that are in the utmost corners, that dwell in the wilderness; for all these nations are uncircumcised, and all the house of Israel are uncircumcised in the heart (Jer 9:26).

Jacob understood by faith that it was only by God's grace that he did not follow the way of Esau and become like those who are of the house of Israel but uncircumcised in heart. For by nature we are children of wrath. But God has had mercy on us.

Jacob's treatment of Esau is instructive. He was continuously kind, not accusing, even though there was reason to wonder about Esau. He considered himself as lowlier than Esau, repeatedly calling him "lord," even though Esau's treatment of him previously had been so bad. Our flesh would rather lash out, or spread rumors, or remind others of what a terrible person someone else is. But this is not the way of the cross. Jacob didn't even gather up a flock to himself to try to defend himself, like Esau did. He just went on in faith and love and hope. Love hopes all things, believes all things, endures all things.

Jacob also did not withhold forgiveness even though God himself had said that Esau was not to inherit the blessing of life. He kept on holding out the hand of forgiveness and peace. Even though he knew what judgment God had spoken against Esau (Gen 27:33), it was not his job to decide if the soil of the heart of an individual person was good soil, or stony ground, or ground parched or by the wayside. He only needed to cast out that good seed of the manna of the Word (Prov 11:24), which is the promises of God that are in Christ Jesus. "That which we have seen and heard declare we unto you, that ye also may have fellowship with us; and truly our fellowship is with the Father, and with his Son Jesus Christ" (1 John 1:3).

www.ingramcontent.com/pod-product-compliance
Lightning Source LLC
Chambersburg PA
CBHW050831160426
43192CB00010B/1978